END TIMES

REVEREND
DEAN CALDWELL

All Scripture quotations are taken from the King James Version of the Bible.

End Times
ISBN: 0-88144-389-1
Copyright © 2009 by Dean Caldwell

Published by
Thorncrown Publishing
A Division of Yorkshire Publishing
9731 East Fifty-Fourth Street
Tulsa, Oklahoma 74146
www.yorkshirepublishing.com

THE COMING OF JESUS

It is important to understand Bible teaching on the coming of the Lord. It is important to understand Bible teaching on the tribulation period, the White Throne Judgment, and hell. These are all part of end-time events. It is also important to understand Bible teaching on the new heaven and the new earth—on what your life is going to be like in those places. Much of the time, we have in our minds that when we get to heaven, all we will be doing is bowing down and worshipping. That will be wonderful and good and we will do those things, but we will be there through eternity and the Scripture explains to us that we're going to assume another life, a very real life according to the Word of God.

To understand end-time events, we must deal with the book of Revelation. The proper way to say that is "Revelation"—it's not "Revelations"—it is Revelation, which means "the end." The book of Revelation is an account of the revealing of things by Christ to John.

Before we dig into Revelation, however, I want you to look at this passage found in 1 Thessalonians 5:1-10:

But of the times and seasons, brethren, ye have no need that I write unto you. For you yourselves know perfectly that the day of the Lord so cometh as a thief in the night. For when they shall say, Peace and safety; then sudden destruction cometh upon them, as travail upon a woman with child; and they shall not escape. But ye, brethren, are not in darkness, that the day should overtake you as a thief. Ye are all the children of light, and the children of the day: we are not of the night, nor of the darkness. Therefore let us not sleep, as others do; but let us watch and be sober. For they that sleep, sleep in the night; and they that be drunken are drunken in the night. But let us, who are of the day, be sober, putting on the breastplate of faith and love; and for a helmet, the hope of salvation. For God hath not appointed us to wrath, but to obtain salvation by our Lord Jesus Christ, who died for us, that, whether we wake or sleep, we should live together with Him.

The coming of the Lord is certain and the Word of God gives us a glimpse into this coming reality in this passage of Scripture. In verse 9, the writer, Paul, tells us that God has not appointed us to wrath but to obtain salvation through our Lord Jesus Christ. All the way through the Word of God from Genesis to the book of Revelation, any time the judgments of God fall, there is always an escape route. God has always provided a way of escape for mankind to be saved out from under and away from the judgments of God. Paul is simply saying here that we, the saved people, the people who are redeemed by the blood of Jesus Christ, we are not appointed to wrath, but to obtain salvation through our Lord Jesus Christ.

There are many passages in Scripture that give us indication that we are in the last days. Here is one that is very powerful. Jesus said in Matthew 24:34, "Verily I say unto you, This generation shall not pass, till all these things be fulfilled." He is simply saying there will be a generation of people on this earth that is going to see the end-time events. These people represent a particular generation, not one scattered over 2,000 years or even over 200 years. There is a particular generation of people that is going to see the end time events take place. I don't know where you stand on this issue, but I believe that we are that generation about which God is speaking.

This brings another question to mind. You may say that a generation is 40 years. Let me correct that and tell you this—a generation is not just confined to 40 years. There are three times in the Scripture that God changed the age span of mankind. From Genesis 1 to Genesis 6, man lived a long, long time. Methuselah lived over 969 years, Noah lived to be 950 and Adam was 930 years old. But then in Genesis 6:3, God says, "My spirit shall not always strive with man, for that he also is flesh." At that point, God determined that man's days would be shortened to 120 years. Then in Psalm 90:10, we read, "that man's days are three score and ten and then ten more with reason of strength." God had now shortend man's days to 70 to 80 years. This is the last time I can find in the Word of God when God mentions determined lifespans and that actually represents the average lifespan today. I know that some reach into their 90's and some over 100 while some pass from this world after only 50 years, but the Bible gives an average span in this passage. With this information in mind, now interpret the words of Jesus when He says

"This generation shall not pass, till all these things be fulfilled" (Matthew 24:34).

There are many things in Scripture to give us insight into the coming of the Lord Jesus. God has marked indicators out and designated to us what we are to look for. The number one sign to look for concerns Israel. All the way through the Word of God, God has instructed us to look at Israel.

The Word of God prophesied that Israel would come together as a nation before the coming of the Lord Jesus Christ. In Amos 9:15, the Lord gave us Israel as a particular sign when He said:

I will plant them upon their land, and they shall no more be pulled up out of their land which I have given them, saith the LORD thy God.

Notice the words, "no more pulled up out of their land." Three times Israel has come back home to their land to declare themselves a nation. Let me recount those three times because when history confirms what is declared in the Word of God, that is very interesting and very assuring to us. The first time Israel came to establish itself as a nation in its own land was when Moses when down to Egypt and brought the Israelites out of Egypt to Canaan. Of course it was not Moses who actually led them into Canaan, that was Joshua, but under the leadership of these men, Israel first possessed the land that God had promised to Abraham, Isaac and Jacob.

After that, the Israelites were scattered because of their idolatry and their disbelief. After many years, Nehemiah, when he rebuilt the walls of Jerusalem, brought them back together a second time and they became a nation again. But once again, they were scattered abroad on the face of the whole earth when they fell into unbelief and doubt and failed to adhere to the things of God.

The third time Israel came back together as a nation was in 1948. Why is the fact that Israel came back home three different times particularly interesting? If you will recall the story of Joseph in Genesis, you may remember that Joseph was sold into slavery by his brothers. Now if you study typology, you will find that Joseph is a type of Christ. Many things in typology will compare things that happened to Joseph to the things that happened to Christ. Joseph was sold by his brothers; Judas sold Christ—both were sold for silver. Joseph had a coat of many colors, Jesus had the scarlet robe. There are many things in typology that will compare Joseph and Christ. Why is that important? Because as we follow the story of Joseph, we see some details that are very important as we study end-time events.

When Joseph wound up in Egypt, Scripture says he was taken from prison and he became second ruler in the nation and he became bread for the country of Egypt. (Six times in John 6, Jesus says, "I am the bread of life.") When Joseph's brothers came back to Egypt for the third time seeking bread, it was at that time that they stayed in Egypt. Upon their third return, Joseph met his brothers in the house and the Word of God says in Genesis 45:1 that, "Joseph put all the Gentiles out of the room and then he made himself known unto his brethren." What does that represent? That is a representation of the rapture of the Church. As Joseph removed the Gentiles from the room, the rapture of the Church will be primarily for the Gentiles—it's for everybody, but it will be primarily for the Gentiles. This is because most of the Jews will not accept Jesus Christ as their

Savior until the tribulation period. It is during the tribulation period when Christ will make Himself known to His brethren.

Another example of typology in the Word of God concerns Noah's Ark. When God was preparing to send judgment on this earth by flooding the earth with water, He told Noah to build an ark for the safety of his house and family. God gave Noah very important, detailed instructions concerning the construction of the ark. God told Noah in Genesis 6:16 that the ark was to be three stories high and the door was to be in the side of the ark. The three stories are a representation of the Father, the Son, and the Holy Ghost. God doesn't do anything just to be doing it. Everything He does has a meaning to it. He didn't just write the Bible to have a thick book. He wrote everything in there because it means something and it translates victory to you and me in our lives.

In looking at the story of Noah and the ark, we find that the door of the ark was in the second story. It was through that door that God preserved mankind. Following the pattern of Father, Son, and Holy Ghost, it was through the side of Jesus Christ that mankind has been preserved through and by the blood of the Lord Jesus Christ. In John 19:34, we learn "that one of the soldiers, with his spear, pierced the side of Jesus, and forthwith came there out both blood and water."

It is amazing to me that the Bible says in Genesis 8:4 that "on the seventh month and on the seventeenth day of the month, the ark came to rest in the mountains of Ararat." The Jewish calendar starts in October. Counting from that point, that means that on April 17, the ark rested. Do you realize that on April 17, Jesus Christ was crucified on the cross of Calvary? Time and again, God's Word reminds us that there is salvation for mankind.

Do you remember when the Israelites were coming from Egypt to Canaan and they crossed over the Red Sea and when they arrived there in the desert they were guided by a cloud by day and a pillar of fire by night? The cloud sheltered them from the sun. There was anywhere from 2 -3 million people in their group—that had to have been a massive cloud to shelter that many from the sun! It's cold in the desert at night, so God built a fire by which His people could warm themselves. He took care of every need they had, but the people still began to complain saying, "We want water, we want water, we have got to have water!"

Moses went to the Lord and said, "These folks need water." The Lord said to him, "Do you see that rock?" We must pay close attention to this rock. The first time God points out this rock, Moses went to the rock, took his staff and smote it—it's very particular in the wording there—he smote the rock on the side and the Bible said water came out of the rock. There was enough to water their flocks and take care of the needs of everybody there—between 2-3 million people. What a wonderful thing it was!

In Numbers 20:8, Moses is sent to that same rock, but this time there is a pronoun included as God says "Speak to the rock and the rock will give forth *his* water." That rock was Christ. Let me prove that to you from the Word of God as we look at 1 Corinthians 10:2-4:

And were all baptized unto Moses in the cloud and in the sea;
and did all eat the same spiritual meat; and did all drink the

same spiritual drink: for they drank of that spiritual Rock that followed them: and that Rock was Christ.

There it is! Right there! That Rock was Christ. I don't know if it scooted or if it moved, I don't know if it rolled or if it appeared and reappeared, but that Rock followed them all the way through the desert.

This knowledge can help clarify what happened when the soldier pierced the side of Christ. As the water and blood poured out, it was more than just water coming out of the sack around His heart. I believe there was an abundance of water and blood because water represents the Word. Notice Ephesians 5:26:

That he might sanctify and cleanse it with the washing of water by the word.

The sanctifying power of God is in the water of the Word. Jesus Christ, our Savior, redeemed us from our sin and we are sanctified by the Word of Almighty God. I'm saved, not because I felt a chill bump, I'm saved because the Word of God said in Romans 10:9: "That if thou shalt confess with thy mouth the Lord Jesus, and shalt believe in thine heart that God hath raised him from the dead, thou shalt be saved." I'm not saved because of what somebody else did, I'm saved because the Word of God declares that I am saved through and by my confession of the Lord Jesus Christ.

I would love to take you all the way through the Old Testament, one typology after another, reflecting on Jesus Christ. He is found all through the Old Testament. I've heard people say, "I don't believe in the Old Testament." Well, we'd better start believing because you can't interpret the New Testament without the Old Testament. You can't interpret the book of Revelation without the book of Daniel. You can't interpret the book of Hebrews without the book of Leviticus. They all tie together. The law that is given in the Old Testament is fulfilled in the flesh of Christ. Everything we preach, everything we teach, everything we sing, whether Old Testament or New, it is all centered around the Savior and the Redeemer of our soul, Jesus Christ, the Lamb of God.

As we continue thinking of the coming of the Lord, keep in mind that there are a lot of things people believe on this subject that just don't bear record. Let me remind you of one of these things that need further needs further explanation. It can be found in Matthew 24:14:

And this gospel of the kingdom shall be preached in all the world for a witness unto all nations; and then shall the end come.

Many people say, "The Lord can't come back because not everybody has heard the Gospel of Jesus Christ." That's not what that Scripture says at all. Everybody is not going to hear the Gospel. Some won't hear it because of choice. Some refuse to hear the Gospel of Jesus Christ. What God is saying in this passage is that He is going to make the Gospel available in every nation on this earth, and it is up to the individual to make the choice to hear and receive. This all goes back to how we were made. We were made with a free will to make choices for ourselves. We choose whether we want to hear or not. We choose whether we want to respond or not.

There will be people who will stand before God and give an account for every ounce of Gospel that's preached from the podium, even though they chose not to attend church anywhere. The Gospel was made available to them, but because of the hardness of their heart they chose not to hear. For this, they are held accountable. God's Word is not just idle words. It will change your life, but if refuse to take it, you are still responsible for your own sin and your own actions. There are people within walking distance of a church who won't bother to darken the door at all because they're not interested and they don't want the Gospel of Jesus Christ, but it is available and it's up to you and up to me to open our ears and receive the things God has for us.

Let's move to some interesting prophecies. Look at the story of the Valley of Dry Bones found in Ezekiel 37:1-14. This is a prophecy God gave that has come to pass in this generation's time.

> *The hand of the LORD was upon me, and carried me out in the spirit of the LORD, and set me down in the midst of the valley which was full of bones, and caused me to pass by them round about: and, behold, there were very many in the open valley; and, lo, they were very dry. And he said unto me, Son of man, can these bones live? And I answered, O Lord GOD, thou knowest.*

> *Again he said unto me, Prophesy upon these bones, and say unto them, O ye dry bones, hear the word of the LORD. Thus saith the Lord GOD unto these bones; Behold, I will cause breath to enter into you, and ye shall live: And I will lay sinews upon you, and will bring up flesh upon you, and cover you with skin, and put breath in you, and ye shall live; and ye shall know that I am the LORD.*

> *So I prophesied as I was commanded: and as I prophesied, there was a noise, and behold a shaking, and the bones came*

together, bone to his bone. And when I beheld, lo, the sinews and the flesh came up upon them, and the skin covered them above: but there was no breath in them.

Then said he unto me, Prophesy unto the wind, prophesy, son of man, and say to the wind, Thus saith the Lord GOD; Come from the four winds, O breath, and breathe upon these slain, that they may live.

So I prophesied as he commanded me, and the breath came into them, and they lived, and stood up upon their feet, an exceeding great army.

Then he said unto me, Son of man, these bones are the whole house of Israel: behold, they say, Our bones are dried, and our hope is lost: we are cut off for our parts. Therefore prophesy and say unto them, Thus saith the Lord GOD; Behold, O my people, I will open your graves, and cause you to come up out of your graves, and bring you into the land of Israel. And ye shall know that I am the LORD, when I have opened your graves, O my people, and brought you up out of your graves, And shall put my spirit in you, and ye shall live, and I shall place you in your own land: then shall ye know that I the LORD have spoken it, and performed it, saith the LORD.

This represents the whole house of Israel. It is not speaking of a revival. This is a prophecy speaking of bringing Israel back home in the 1930's—1940's after the Jews were brutally killed in Germany by the hand of Hitler and also brutally persecuted by Mussolini. The European Jews were under such attack by the enemy throughout Europe that they began to go back home. That's what this prophecy is all about. God says, "There is a finger bone on this side of the valley and a hand bone over here." Then the finger bone started flopping and the hand bone started moving and they came together and before long, the valley was full of skeletons just laying there as Israel came home to that barren wasteland they called home. Nobody wanted this area of land at that time. It was seen as junk land, there was nothing there. But God had a plan. He had a plan for that area.

When Israel came home, they were dry and hopeless, but Ezekiel prophesied the second time and when he did, flesh and sinews came upon the bones. Do you realize that Israel has become one of the most prosperous nations on the globe? They're exporting food and they're the #1 exporter of roses in this world! Why is this important? Because Isaiah 35:1 says that "this place will blossom as the rose." Isaiah 35:6 says "there will be streams in the desert."

Isaiah 35:8 says "there's a highway in that desert called the highway of holiness and, the unclean shall not pass over it... the wayfaring men, though fools, shall not err therein." Let me explain this scripture—that highway will be there during the Millennial Reign. It will be a designated highway that the unclean are just not allowed to walk on. That blesses me to my bones because there's been so much I have been left out of because I'm a preacher. There has been so much I haven't been invited to because I'm a Christian. But when Christ reigns, there will be designated areas that I can go in that others cannot! These are in place by the designation of our Lord Jesus Christ and we'll rule and reign with Him.

In Ezekiel 37:10, we see that Ezekiel prophesied a third time and breath came and these once-dry bones stood on their feet, an exceeding great army. In 1967, when Israel went to war with Egypt, a nation 10 times its size, in just a matter of days Egypt was ready for the war to end. This was to fulfill the prophecy that God gave through the rest of Ezekiel 37.

There are some great things coming and God says this generation shall not pass until these things be fulfilled. The Word of God says the temple is going to be rebuilt. The Word of God says that Israel will resume their sacrifices one more time. Let me let you in on a little secret: Did you know that they have already found the four cornerstones of the temple? These huge stones are each 8 to 10 feet thick and 8 to 16 feet long. They were originally put in place by slave labor by bringing in baskets of dirt and laying it down then dragging the stone in over top of this dirt. When the temple was torn down in 70 AD, the stones were removed the same way, that's why this area is called the temple mound. This massive piece of land was just covered up by dirt. Israel has already started pre-fabricating the temple on this piece of land. They have already made the golden Menorah at the cost of $3 million. They have made the shewbread table as well. It has already been built.

In July of 2008, there were already 126 who had signed up to study in the priesthood. Through DNA testing, they have been able to determine who is of the tribe of Levi. It seems they have discovered that the Levites have an extra gene that the rest of the Israelites don't have. Isn't it amazing how God has preserved all of this? Currently, they are measuring these 126 Levites for their priestly robes. The robes have to be made by hand and they have to be made to fit. They can't be ordered from a catalog—everything has to be perfect. These people are preparing and believing that they will soon return to the sacrificial system. Several years ago in the state of

Mississippi, they found the red cows and they shipped them to Israel. They've been raising red cattle over in Israel for some time.

In the last part of 2006, the caves where the Dead Sea Scrolls were discovered were re-explored. One of the soldiers in the expedition leaned up against, what would be found to be, a false wall and fell through. When he fell through the false wall, he found a rock table there with a rock cross with an inscription that read, "The continued ashes…." The more time that passes, the more things are coming together just as God said they would. When God says something is going to come to pass, you can be assured it is going to happen just as the Word of God declares.

All of this points toward another time and another place when the trumpet of God is going to sound and when it does, those who are looking for Him, who have made themselves ready, will leave here in a moment, in the twinkling of an eye.

We can't talk about the rapture of the Church without looking at 1 Thessalonians 4:13-18:

> *But I would not have you to be ignorant, brethren, concerning them which are asleep, that ye sorrow not, even as others which have no hope. For if we believe that Jesus died and rose again, even so them also which sleep in Jesus will God bring with him. For this we say unto you by the word of the Lord, that we which are alive and remain unto the coming of the Lord shall not prevent them which are asleep.*
>
> *For the Lord himself shall descend from heaven with a shout, with the voice of the archangel, and with the trump of God: and the dead in Christ shall rise first: Then we which are alive and remain shall be caught up together with them in the*

clouds, to meet the Lord in the air: and so shall we ever be with the Lord.

Wherefore comfort one another with these words.

Paul said there will be a time when the trumpet of God is going to sound and the dead in Christ are going to rise first. This has been interpreted to mean that the dead in Christ are going to rise first because they are six feet underneath us, but there is a big problem with this thinking. What about those who died at sea? What about those who burned to death? What about those who were eaten by animals so that nothing was left to bury? The dead in Christ rising first has nothing to do with how deep they're buried or whether they're buried or not. The dead in Christ will rise first because they will be the first ones to know about the rapture of the Church.

You see, your loved ones who passed away, when they closed their eyes in mortal death, were very much alive and well when they passed into the presence of God. Let me give you a family report on that—everything is going well, they are doing great. They are in the presence of God. They're not comatose. They are very much alive and they are very well and before the rapture, before the trumpet of God sounds, He's going to gather all the saints together. Verse 14, confirms this when it says, "them also which sleep in Jesus will God bring with him." Those who have died in Christ are in the presence of God. 2 Corinthians 5:8 tells us "that to be absent from this body is to be present with God." They are in the presence of God right now, but before the rapture of the Church takes place, God will gather them together and say, "I'm going to put you back on this earth, but you're not going to stay there. I'm going to give you a brand new body." Right now, they are soul and spirit, but when the trumpet sounds, they will receive a brand new body. At that time, we who are alive and remain will be changed and we will receive an incorruptible body as well.

Consider 1 Corinthians 15:51-57:

Behold, I shew you a mystery; We shall not all sleep, but we shall all be changed, in a moment, in the twinkling of an eye, at the last trump: for the trumpet shall sound, and the dead shall be raised incorruptible, and we shall be changed.

For this corruptible must put on incorruption, and this mortal must put on immortality. So when this corruptible shall have put on incorruption, and this mortal shall have put on immortality, then shall be brought to pass the saying that is written, Death is swallowed up in victory. O death, where is thy sting? O grave, where is thy victory?

The sting of death is sin; and the strength of sin is the law. But thanks be to God, which giveth us the victory through our Lord Jesus Christ.

We will receive a brand new body. For those who are sleeping in the grave, their body is in the grave but their inner man is in the presence of God and God will bring them back. That is what the scripture in 1 Thessalonians 4 is saying—the dead will rise first not because they're buried below us but because they will be the first to know about the rapture of the Church. Then those who remain will join them and together will rise with them to meet the Lord of Glory in the air and so shall we ever be with the Lord! What a God and what a plan that God has!

The rapture of the Church is an event that is going to take place and I believe that you and I are the generation He is speaking of when He said "when you see these things come to pass, this generation shall not pass till all these things be fulfilled." The prophecies recorded in Matthew 24, Luke 21, and all that we see in the Old Testament book of Daniel—all of the things are coming to pass on this earth and I believe that the rapture of the Church is the dividing point of the tribulation period.

There seems to be so much controversy in the church world over when the rapture of the Church will come—before the tribulation period, during the tribulation period or after the tribulation period. Many times, students of the Bible get hung up on this issue. A preacher once told me that he couldn't have a Bible study on the rapture of the Church because there were so many diverse beliefs in his church, the study would get tied up and out of hand. I told him I could help him with his problem simply by turning to the Word. When the Word of God speaks on an issue, all other beliefs must cease. I referred this pastor to Revelation 4:1:

After this I looked, and, behold, a door was opened in heaven: and the first voice which I heard was as it were of a trumpet talking with me; which said, Come up hither, and I will shew thee things which must be hereafter.

In this passage, John has finished recording the words to the seven churches mentioned in Revelation 2 and 3 and now in chapter 4, we see all of the elements of a rapture accounted for: a trumpet sounding, a door opening, and a rising. Before the first seal, the first vial, or the first scroll is opened, there's an indication of the rapture of the Church.

Now look over at Revelation 7:9, 14:

After this I beheld, and, lo, a great multitude, which no man could number, of all nations, and kindreds, and people, and tongues, stood before the throne, and before the Lamb, clothed with white robes, and palms in their hands...These are they which came out of great tribulation, and have washed their robes, and made them white in the blood of the Lamb.

This passage speaks of people leaving during the tribulation period, between the 6th and 7th seal. This is in the Bible—you just read it for yourself—people are going to leave during the tribulation period.

Now look at Revelation 20:4:

And I saw thrones, and they sat upon them, and judgment was given unto them: and I saw the souls of them that were beheaded for the witness of Jesus, and for the word of God, and which had not worshipped the beast, neither his image, neither had received his mark upon their foreheads, or in their hands; and they lived and reigned with Christ a thousand years.

This passage speaks of a group that has gone all the way through the tribulation period. How do we know that? It says they did not bow to the beast or his image and they were persecuted because of the Word of God. We know that taking the mark of the beast is not recorded as mandatory until chapter 13 and chapter 17 of the book of Revelation, which takes place during the second half of the tribulation period. The group spoken of in this passage does not receive the mark of the beast. They go all the way through the tribulation period until they give their lives for the cause of Christ.

Each of these scriptures could be used to support whatever position you may choose to hold on when the rapture of the Church may take place. The point I'm making is, why fuss about such matters? Why argue and fight about this? All three opinions are supported by scripture. The important question is, which group are you going to go with? There's going to be a rapture of the Church before the tribulation period ever starts. If you want to go, get ready and be looking for Christ. If you want to go halfway through the tribulation, hang on, it's gonna be a bumpy ride. And if you think you're going to go all the way through the tribulation period, and there are some that will, there is scripture that can verify that position. The important question is what are you doing to prepare for the coming of Christ? His return is going to happen. What are you doing to make sure that others are prepared for His return?

Jesus is coming—we are that generation He spoke about. Jesus Christ is coming just like the Word declares. God said no man knows the day or the hour. He didn't put a time on it, He just said it's going to happen. Are you ready?

TRIBULATION AND GREAT TRIBULATION

Revelation chapters 4 through 18 give details concerning the tribulation period. To properly understand these details, we will look first to Matthew 24 because that chapter is perfectly divided up for us: the first 14 verses contain prophecy about the end times; verses 15-28 speak about the Great Tribulation period; verses 29-35 concern Christ's coming after the tribulation period; verses 36-44 speak about the unexpected coming of the Lord; and finally, verses 45-51 talk about the wise and the foolish servants. I want to direct your attention to Matthew 24:29-31 as these verses concern tribulation and the Great Tribulation.

Immediately after the tribulation of those days shall the sun be darkened, and the moon shall not give her light, and the stars shall fall from heaven, and the powers of the heavens shall be shaken: And then shall appear the sign of the Son of man in heaven: and then shall all the tribes of the earth mourn, and they shall see the Son of man coming in the clouds of heaven with power and great glory. And he shall send his angels with a great sound of a trumpet, and they

*shall gather together his elect from the four winds, from one
end of heaven to the other.*

Let's begin by working toward a better understanding of the
book of Revelation—how it is divided, the details of how things are
going to happen and what is going to come to pass. The tribulation
period refers to a specific seven year period that is divided into two
parts: three and one-half years as described in the first part of
Revelation and then another three and one-half years which is
referred to as "Great Tribulation." In Matthew 24:29, the period is
divided for us. The writer of Matthew says, "Immediately after the
tribulation of those days...." Then notice his next words, "the sun
will be darkened, the moon shall not give her light and the stars shall
fall." This is a specific event described to us in the Word of God.

Let me divide the book of Revelation up for you. I know there
are many resources that go into this at length, but let me just show
you the simplicity of the Word of God and what it plainly says. In
Revelation 1:19, God clearly divides the book into three different
sections. He tells John:

*Write the things which thou hast seen, and the things which
are, and the things which shall be hereafter;*

John is told first to write what he has seen and only things he had
seen to that point are recorded in Revelation 1. Second, John is told
to write the things which are. These things are detailed in Revelation
2 and 3 which contains the information on the seven churches. Then
John is told to write the things which shall be hereafter. This section
stretches from Revelation 4 to Revelation 22.

It is my personal belief that I won't be around to have to know anything after Revelation chapter 3, but if you plan to stay around for events detailed beyond chapter 3, there are a few things you will need to know. When I pastored in Whitehall, I built a little box in the back of the church and I put a cassette tape in the box on which was recorded my sermon on 15 things to do if you miss the rapture of the Church. I also put a New Testament in the box with the tape. I posted a sign that read, "In case of the rapture, break this glass." I kept that box in the back of the church. Since no one ever broke the glass, I decided that God hadn't come yet and we moved right along.

John is told to write the things that he had seen and he does so in the introduction to the book of Revelation. Revelation 1:1-3 explains what the entire book is about. John tells us that this book is the revelation of Jesus Christ, revealed. Please understand, before Jesus went to the cross, rose from the grave and then spent 40 days with His disciples, he told them "seal this up" meaning to seal up all that the disciples had seen. But now He is giving this revelation to the disciples. In 96 AD, the book of Revelation that we have in our possession was given to the Apostle John on the Isle of Patmos. God is not only wanting us to understand this revelation, but this is the only book in the Bible that specifically says you are blessed if you read it. I know there are a lot of people who don't want to read Revelation because they feel it is too difficult to understand. I can understand that sentiment because there has been so much debate on the message and meaning of the book, so many different perspectives, that you can stay confused if you're not careful. But God lays things out plainly if you will only follow His direction in studying the book of Revelation. I hope that by reading this book, you will have a clear understanding of this book of the Bible. It is so important that we do because our world needs to know what's going to come upon this earth. The message of Revelation may frighten you but it will also make you live better, more righteous before God, when you understand what is going to come upon this earth.

The salutation is given to us in Revelation 1:4-6. The theme of Revelation is given to us in Revelation 1:7-8. John the prophet is described in Revelation 1:9-11. John's vision of Jesus Christ is given in Revelation 1:12-18.

In verses 19-20, you are given the divisions and the symbols. What John saw, in general, was Jesus walking among the seven candlesticks and in verse 20, John describes what that is. He says the stars are the angels of the churches and the candlesticks are the churches. What does that indicate? There never was a "day" of revival—but there has always been "a God of revival" and He still walks among the churches today. Everything that God said in His Word that He would do still applies today.

To understand how important that is, let me point out a very powerful scripture that doesn't get much attention. Look at Hebrews 13:8:

Jesus Christ the same yesterday, and to day, and for ever.

That literally means that I can know what He's going to be like tomorrow. I know what He's going to be like next week—based on His history and what He has done in the present. Jesus Christ is the same yesterday—that's history. He's the same today. And forever— you can be assured in your heart and your mind that nothing in the power of God has changed in the history, in the present, or in the future of mankind. You can count on it. If He'll save and deliver in the 40's and 50's, He'll do it today and He'll be saving and delivering tomorrow. If He healed the sick in the 50's and the 60's, He'll do the same today. If He did that then, if you get up in the morning or next week, you can count on the fact that He is the Savior, the Healer, the Baptizer, and every promise in the Word of God is for you and me. As Jesus was walking among His Church then, He is still doing today.

Secondly, John saw and heard from heaven the things which are. This was the second division of the book of Revelation containing information that applies until the rapture of the Church. Seven characteristics of the seven churches are given to us in the Word of God. These seven churches were Gentile churches. I know there are some people who like to take the information on the seven churches and divide it up into seven dispensational periods of time. Possibly, that perspective has merit, but more importantly for us, I believe that all seven characteristics and spirits of those churches still exist today. They are represented in the congregations of our church world right here and now. It's not something that is history, this concerns things which are. You and I are living in chapter 2 and chapter 3 of the book of Revelation. To see where we are today, begin by looking at Revelation 1:9-20:

> *I John, who also am your brother, and companion in tribulation, and in the kingdom and patience of Jesus Christ, was in the isle that is called Patmos, for the word of God, and for the testimony of Jesus Christ.*
>
> *I was in the Spirit on the Lord's day, and heard behind me a great voice, as of a trumpet, Saying, I am Alpha and*

Omega, the first and the last: and, What thou seest, write in a book, and send it unto the seven churches which are in Asia; unto Ephesus, and unto Smyrna, and unto Pergamos, and unto Thyatira, and unto Sardis, and unto Philadelphia, and unto Laodicea.

And I turned to see the voice that spake with me. And being turned, I saw seven golden candlesticks; and in the midst of the seven candlesticks one like unto the Son of man, clothed with a garment down to the foot, and girt about the paps with a golden girdle. His head and his hairs were white like wool, as white as snow; and his eyes were as a flame of fire; and his feet like unto fine brass, as if they burned in a furnace; and his voice as the sound of many waters.

And he had in his right hand seven stars: and out of his mouth went a sharp two edged sword: and his countenance was as the sun shineth in his strength.

And when I saw him, I fell at his feet as dead. And he laid his right hand upon me, saying unto me, Fear not; I am the first and the last: I am he that liveth, and was dead; and, behold, I am alive for evermore, Amen; and have the keys of hell and of death.

Write the things which thou hast seen, and the things which are, and the things which shall be hereafter;

The mystery of the seven stars which thou sawest in my right hand, and the seven golden candlesticks. The seven stars are the angels of the seven churches: and the seven candlesticks which thou sawest are the seven churches.

Starting with chapter 2, John begins to describe the churches. The church at Ephesus was a few miles from the Aegean Sea on the Cayster River. One of the wonders of this time was found there—the

Temple of Artemis. The Romans called this the Temple of Diana. The worship there included shameless and vile practices such as prostitution and sexual rituals. That same spirit is dominating in our world today. It is alive and real. The Lord chose seven churches for His revelation and each one of them had a different characteristic about it. You can see all of them flowing in the church world today.

The second church mentioned was Smyrna. It is very important to know where these churches were located. Smyrna was one of the most beautiful cities in all Asia. It is located in modern Izmir, Turkey. The people in Smyrna knew about God but they had turned their back on Him.

The third church was in Pergamos. Pergamos was a capitol city of Asia. There were two capitols at this time—Rome and Pergamos. Pergamos was also called the seat of Satan. In the book of Daniel, chapter 2, we read that Nebuchadnezzar saw a great statue that had a head of gold, a belly of silver, a bottom of brass, and legs of iron. The two legs represented these two capitols with feet made of iron and clay. The people of Pergamos were very idolatrous in nature. The god of Baal was being worshipped there and the doctrine of Baalam was being practiced. You may remember the story of Baalam from Numbers 22 through 25. Baalam was summoned by king Balak to curse the children of Israel. When Baalam looked down upon them, he said that he could not curse the children of Israel because "they had the shout of a king in their midst." But though he could not curse Israel, Baalam did advise the king to have the Moabite women come to seduce the men of Israel and that's how they would be brought down. What he suggested is exactly what took place. How does that apply to us today? When the world begins to infiltrate the church, you can always expect a fall spiritually. God help us to keep our prayer life and the Word of God on the front burner of our soul that we might be spiritually fit to be used in the glorious kingdom of God.

Thyatira was the fourth church mentioned. This was just a little town in importance, but the Lord included it to be mentioned among the other cities because Thyatira was noted for its adulterous acts. This city had Jezebel who was in the fortune telling business. She was telling them it was acceptable to commit fornication and partake of offerings that were offered to idols. Jezebel's teaching had infiltrated the church world.

Pay special attention to this scripture that we find in 2 Thessalonians 2:3:

> *Let no man deceive you by any means: for that day shall not come, except there come a falling away first, and that man of sin be revealed, the son of perdition;*

We don't want to focus on the falling away, but this reality does exist. It is spoken of in the Word of God. But in the same mention as the falling away, we see in Acts 2:16-21:

> *But this is that which was spoken by the prophet Joel; And it shall come to pass in the last days, saith God, I will pour out of my Spirit upon all flesh: and your sons and your daughters shall prophesy, and your young men shall see visions, and your old men shall dream dreams: and on my servants and on my handmaidens I will pour out in those days of my Spirit; and they shall prophesy:*

And I will shew wonders in heaven above, and signs in the earth beneath; blood, and fire, and vapour of smoke: The sun shall be turned into darkness, and the moon into blood, before the great and notable day of the Lord come: And it shall come to pass, that whosoever shall call on the name of the Lord shall be saved.

Do you see how the tribulation period connects in this passage from Acts? God's Word is cohesive. It ties together. At the same time that there is a falling away, there is going to be an outpouring of the Spirit of God. That doesn't mean that there is a contradiction in the Word of God, it simply means that we have a choice.

This falling away is a spiritual matter, not numerical. We're living in a world today that has more mega-churches than there has ever been in the history of the church world, but yet when we have to sit down and counsel and explain why God didn't do what His Word said He would do, we cannot do so honestly. That's a falling away. We try to explain away why God didn't do what His Word said He would do. Why don't we just swallow the lump in our throat, square our shoulders and look people in the eye and admit we're not praying, we're not reading and we're not fasting and we're not where we need to be spiritually with God to bring to pass the things God said He would do. That's the falling away that He's talking about. Our unwillingness to do what God commands to bring His Word to pass in our world.

How many of you have been hearing about Pentecost for 30 years? We are a generation that knows exactly what we're talking about when we talk about the power of the living God. I've lived through an era of time when I've seen people get out of wheelchairs and walk. I've seen blind eyes opened, I've seen deaf mutes healed. I've seen this with my own eyes. A few years ago, I was preaching on healing and I gave a few testimonies. A brother came to me and asked if all I said was documented. He said that I needed to document those miracles I had witnessed. This made me aggravated. This was my brother in the Lord saying these things! I thought, *Has it come to the point where people don't even believe that God can do these things, or that God will do them?* Do we have to document everything? Is it not enough for us to tell people that God says He can and then believe that He will? No matter how big your stories about God, you need never lie because God is bigger than your imagination and He is greater than your dream and He can do more than you expect Him to do. He's that kind of God. The falling away is when we get to the point that we have to explain why God did not do what His Word says He will do. But the good news is that at the same time we see this falling away, there is an outpouring of the Spirit of God.

Next we go to the church at Sardis. It was located on the slopes of the mountains. It was a very great city that existed for more than 2,000 years. It was in such a location that the residents were able to defend the city from all forces that came their way. This city was something to behold, but the church was dead and formal. The reason the city was eventually destroyed was because the residents got to the point that they felt they were impregnable so they let their army diminish and when they did, the enemy came in and overthrew them and tore their city down. I believe that in much of the church world today, we are at that point. We believe nothing can bring us down. We've let our guard down and when you let your guard down, the enemy will hit you with everything he can. We need to stay alive and alert with the Word of Almighty God.

Let me reassure you, the Word will do everything that it says it will do. It is the Word of Almighty God. Look at Hebrews 4:12:

For the word of God is quick, and powerful, and sharper than any two edged sword, piercing even to the dividing asunder of soul and spirit, and of the joints and marrow, and is a discerner of the thoughts and intents of the heart.

The Word of God is a separator and a divider. Anytime the Word of God is mentioned in scripture, it is referred to as a sword or water. A few times in scripture, the Word of God is referred to as a two-edged, or double edged sword. What makes the double edge on the Word of God? If you study the original Greek this becomes clearer. This double edge comes when "you say what God has already said." This is important because God has established His Word. In Matthew 24:35, Jesus says, "Heaven and earth shall pass away, but my words shall not pass away." When I say what God has already said, I'm putting the double edge on that sword. When the enemy comes against me, I get the Word out and I say like Jesus said in Matthew 4, "It is written...." When Jesus said what God had already said, the devil left Him. I want you to remember that. If you're battling something in your life—a disease, an affliction, a problem—say what God has said. Put the double edge on the sword!

Next we come to the church at Philadelphia. It was located in a region that had volcanic activity. The city was almost destroyed by earthquake several times, but it survived. This is also recorded as the church with brotherly love. As is true of every church that we read about in Revelation, you can find this characteristic in the church world today.

Finally, we come to the church of Laodicea. Laodicea was noted for its commerce and its banking. It was a tourist center that had hot mineral baths. The Laodiceans were also manufacturers of a special ointment that was widely sought after. But the members of this church were not dedicated or committed to Christ. Today, there are statistics that say that a church member can miss 17 Sundays a year and still be counted as faithful. That's the new definition of faithful. It's amazing how we have lowered the standard down through the years to accommodate people. We have failed to look at what accommodates God in our worship and our time of reflecting on Him. Standards have been lowered in the church world and in society in general. We see this in our schools. When I went to school, 95-100% was an "A," then it went down from there. Schools have now lowered the grade scale so they can have more "A" students and more "B" students. If I went to school now, I'd be a whiz! We have made these accommodations to make the quantity look good but the quality is dropping.

To the church at Laodicea Christ says in Revelation 3:20:

Behold, I stand at the door, and knock: if any man hear my voice, and open the door, I will come in to him, and will sup with him, and he with me.

This is the only time in scripture that you'll find Jesus standing outside the church knocking on the door trying to get in. He made a promise to come in if you'll open the door, but what does that mean? Remember, we're in the midst of a falling away and an outpouring of the Spirit at the same time. Those who want an outpouring have to open the door and let Christ in. He's not going to force His way in, you've got to invite Him in and you've got to allow Him to be God of everything that you are.

In Exodus 20, God lays out the Ten Commandments. In verse 3, God commands "that we are to have no other gods before Him." If there weren't many, many gods, He wouldn't have written that. I believe the Ten Commandments are written in prioritized order. I believe this is true because Jesus said time and again in the New Testament, "The greatest of these...." In Ephesians 4:5, we are told there is "One Lord, one faith, one baptism." There are many gods, but there is just one Lord. A god is anything you worship and you can worship anywhere you want to whenever you have time. But when you make God "Lord of your life," that indicates ownership. That means He now has priority in your life. He is sitting on the throne of your heart. There is a difference between just looking at Him as God and looking at Him as Lord God. There is a difference that comes as He sits on the throne of your heart and takes owner-ship of your life.

Following the discussion of the churches, the third division of the book of Revelation takes us into the tribulation period as it goes into things that must be hereafter. In chapter 4 of the book of Revelation a door is opened, a throne is seen, and the four and twenty elders are spoken about. We read of scenes of heavenly worship. In chapter 5, you'll find the sealed book and the Lamb that prevails to open the book. In chapter 5 we also hear of the worship of God and the Lamb.

When you get to Revelation chapters 6 and 7, we begin to read about the seals, the trumpets and the vials. This is a where we see the rise of an anti-Christ. When the first seal is opened in Revelation 6, there are four horses that ride. There's a white horse, a red horse, a black horse and a pale horse. All four of these horses stand for something and you must read carefully to understand. For example, the white horse that rides in Revelation 6 is the anti-Christ but the white horse that rides in Revelation 19 is THE Christ. Don't be confused. The anti-Christ rides on the white horse with a bow in his hand and he goes out to conquer. He has no arrows, he just has a bow. This indicates that he has no military at that time. He's just man who is going to come in with flattery.

For confirmation of this, we can look to Daniel 7 where Daniel saw his vision of the beast that rose up with seven heads and ten horns around the neck of the beast. On this beast, there is also a little horn that represents the anti-Christ. In Daniel 7:8, we see that three of the horns are plucked up by the roots. When you look at Daniel 7 and Revelation 6, the word "anti-Christ" and the word "beast" refer to the same person but they are different personalities. The personality changes when it mentions the three horns that are plucked up by the roots. These three horns refer to three nations that the anti-Christ will bankrupt financially and undermine politically. Once he bankrupts these nations, he will conquer them. Keep in mind, the anti-Christ has no military. He has a bow, but he has no arrow. You might beat somebody to death with a bow, but you're not going to do any shooting because without an arrow, there is no military backing at all. The anti-Christ just has the bow, he has no military behind him. But once he conquers those three nations, then he will have control of the military of those three nations and that will be very intimidating to the world.

Now that the anti-Christ is armed with a military, the first three and one-half years of the tribulation period will be filled with constant war. Matthew 24 tells us that nation will rise against nation and kingdom against kingdom. At this point, the anti-Christ starts battling and his personality changes from anti-Christ to beast because of his brutality. He has now become possessed by the dragon. Let's look at that together in Revelation 13:2:

> *And the beast which I saw was like unto a leopard, and his feet were as the feet of a bear, and his mouth as the mouth of a lion: and the dragon gave him his power, and his seat, and great authority.*

Notice these three appearances—the leopard, the bear and the lion—they come together as one beast who is very brutal in his tactics.

From Revelation 13, we enter the last half of the tribulation period. The first half is to be filled with all kinds of wars but then a treaty is going to be made with Israel which probably will entail giving them free reign to perform their sacrifices and their rituals. As the first three and one half years end, the anti-Christ will show his true colors when, at that time, he breaks his covenant with Israel. Israel will then leave their land and flee for their lives and the 144,000 will be sealed. When it mentions the 144,000 Jews who are sealed by the Spirit of God, notice that the tribe of Dan and the tribe of Ephraim are not there. They are substituted. Why? The book of Deuteronomy and the book of Leviticus give us insight. The tribe of Dan and the tribe of Ephraim were the ones who brought idolatry to the nation of Israel and they were rejected by God. You will find, however, that these tribes are accounted for in the Millennial Reign. They will go through the tribulation period and pay the debt for the sin of their past. That may raise eyebrows, but that's how it's laid out to us in the Word of God.

The last half of the tribulation period is called Great Tribulation. When you hear of that, you can know that everything is intensified during that time. The devil knows he's running out of time and he intends to focus all his remaining power through the anti-Christ. The anti-Christ is now referred to as the beast as in Revelation 13:5 when the forty and two months are spoken of and then in Revelation 13:8 when it says that "all will worship him whose names are not written in the book of life." These are also the people who are going to die in the battle of Armageddon, those who have received the mark of the beast.

When the anti-Christ comes into power, he will come with flattery and deception. Many people believe that the anti-Christ will just announce that he is in charge, but that's not the case. There will still be other world orders and governments, but this man is going to come in with all of his answers and all of his flattery and solve the problems of the nations, the whole time gaining the support of the world behind him. They will follow him. We're headed toward that one-world system right now. We are not the only ones on this planet with an economic crisis. Every nation right now is worried about their economic system. They're meeting and trying to find answers.

When you read Revelation and read about the trumpets, the seals, and the vials, know that many of these events are going to be happening simultaneously. Though there are chapters that describe the seals and then chapters that describe the trumpets and then chapters that describe the vials, many of these events will happen simultaneously.

Returning to the descriptions of the four horses in Revelation, the red horse that rides is war—kingdom against kingdom. The black horse is famine. When all able bodied men are drafted and there's no one left to do any sowing or reaping, famine is going to be on this globe like you've never seen before. The pale horse represents death. You find in Revelation 6 that it says that "one fourth of the world's population will die from famine and war." This is all during the first half of the tribulation period.

When the first trumpet begins to bring in the second half of the tribulation, the Great Tribulation period, the Lord is going to repeat the plagues of Egypt. You can find these plagues recorded in the book of Exodus and in the book of Revelation.

The Great Tribulation ends with the seventh trump, the seventh seal, and the seventh vial. After the Great Tribulation, the one hour judgments will occur. This is found in Revelation 18:10:

Standing afar off for the fear of her torment, saying, Alas, alas that great city Babylon, that mighty city! for in one hour is thy judgment come.

There are three Babylons that are mentioned here: a political Babylon, an economic Babylon, and a religious Babylon. All of these represent an anti-Christ spirit. In this verse, it says that Babylon will fall. This is a rebuilt Babylon that will fall in one hour's time. Look now at Revelation 18:17, 19:

> *For in one hour so great riches is come to nought. And every shipmaster, and all the company in ships, and sailors, and as many as trade by sea, stood afar off,*
>
> *And they cast dust on their heads, and cried, weeping and wailing, saying, Alas, alas that great city, wherein were made rich all that had ships in the sea by reason of her costliness! for in one hour is she made desolate.*

This one hour judgment is a devastating earthquake that is going to take place and it will destroy the rebuilt Babylon. Not only that, but it will divide Jerusalem into three parts and 7,000 men alone will die in Jerusalem in this great earthquake. In one hour along with this great earthquake, there will be hail that will fall from heaven that is identified as weighing a talent. Keep in mind, a talent weighs between 90-100 pounds. This will be devastation like this world has never seen before or will see again. The one hour judgments that are coming on this earth will certainly take place as God's Word says they will. They will happen.

What will signal the coming of this earthquake to start the one hour judgments? Revelation 11 tells us that in the last half of the tribulation period, God will send two witnesses to this earth. They will witness 1,260 days. They are coming down from heaven and they are going to witness on this earth. Nothing can kill them and nothing can harm them until the appointed time. When that time comes, they will be killed. After the witnesses have been killed and their bodies left in the streets for three and one half days, then life will return to them and they will rise again and be called up to heaven. Look with me at Revelation 11:13:

And the same hour was there a great earthquake, and the tenth part of the city fell, and in the earthquake were slain of men seven thousand: and the remnant were affrighted, and gave glory to the God of heaven.

This is the beginning of the one hour judgments. The earthquake is going to come.

Why would God send these witnesses to earth? As we get closer to the end of time, more and more people are giving God less and less credit for anything. It doesn't make any difference what God does, it is explained away, His handiwork is not talked about, never acknowledged. God is denied, put down, trampled on. His Name is in defeat in the minds of a lot of people. The truth is, His Name is victorious, people just refuse to acknowledge it! But they will. In the last half of the Great Tribulation period, these two witnesses are going to wreak havoc on this earth. In the Name of the Lord, these witnesses will call down the plagues upon the earth. There will be no denying what is happening. You won't be able to call it global warming or give any other explanation. For three and one half years, these witnesses are going to declare the plagues of God on planet earth and there will be no one who can argue or deny it. The Bible says "they will smite this earth as oft as they will." That means they will be given full reign and full power and they are going to call the plagues down on this earth one right after another in the Name of the Lord. When they say "tomorrow there will be lice"—there will be lice the next day. The plagues will be repeated in a bigger form than when they first came upon Egypt. As the Jews in Egypt were shielded from the plagues, the 144,000 Jews sealed by God will likewise be shielded from these plagues.

The Bible tells us that these two witnesses cannot be killed for 1,260 days. In Revelation 11:7, it says, "when they shall have finished their testimony...." What happens then? The beast that has come from the pit makes war against them and kills them and they lay in the street and the world is so glad they are dead that they celebrate. The people of earth will send gifts back and forth to one another to celebrate the fact that the guys who were making havoc are now dead. Little do they know that the one hour judgment is coming and then the KING OF KINGS AND LORD OF LORDS will descend from heaven and bring an end to it all.

You may wonder why God has kept you in this world. Let me tell you why: You have not finished your testimony. When you were saved and you gave your heart and life to Jesus, not only did you give Him your life, you gave Him the ending of your life. That explains the scripture that says that "He is the author and the finisher of our faith." That scripture has nothing to do with eternity because there's no finish in eternity. It has everything to do with right now. As long as you're living and you have breath, you're still an oracle that God can use for His glory and honor. You may wonder how God can get any glory when His people are suffering. The fact is, suffering or no, God is still calling the shots. He's the Alpha and Omega, the beginning and the ending, the author and the finisher of our faith. If I die tomorrow, it is because God has gotten all the glory out of me He can get. And He will receive glory and honor from my departure from this earth as well. Not only does God leave people here to show you how to live in faith, He lets some people show you how to die in faith as well. It's important that we know we're in the hands of Almighty God and He has your best interest in mind.

This great earthquake mentioned in Revelation 6, 11, 12, 16, and 18, is so great it will level mountains. It will raise the Dead Sea to such an extent that it will flow into the Red Sea (Ezekiel 47:1-12). It will destroy the rebuilt Babylon. It will divide Jerusalem into three parts. And then the great hail will come.

We're hearing about things coming together as a one nation, one world order. This is outlined in the Word of God. We are told there will be a world government. There will be a world court system. There will be a world police force. There will be a world commerce. There will be a world bank. There will be a world measurement. There will be a world communication and language. And there will be a world church. Some of these things we can see forming and some have already formed in our time. All of this is foretold in the Word of God as leading up to the Great Tribulation period and then the one hour judgment which leads us up to Revelation 19 and the second coming of Jesus Christ.

If you have family who do not know the Lord, spend more time in prayer for them. Pray that God will open their eyes to see, their ears to hear, their mind to understand that we're in the last of the last days. We need to get busy and become more faithful. Quit being so discouraged and start encouraging other people. We come to church looking to be uplifted, but we need to be coming to lift God up, declaring that our God reigns and He is on the throne. He is the soon coming King, the beginning and the ending, and He has something for me to do for the kingdom of Almighty God.

The events of the tribulation are going to happen as outlined in both the Old and New Testaments in God's Word. Understanding the end times can make a difference to you, but what is truly important is reinforced in Hebrews 9:27-28:

And as it is appointed unto men once to die, but after this the judgment: So Christ was once offered to bear the sins of many; and unto them that look for him shall he appear the second time without sin unto salvation.

The "look for him" is key. We must look for Him, be ready for Him. It seems that now more than ever, talking about the end times and the rapture of the Church is a controversial subject—even within the body of believers. Speaking about these things is considered "scare tactics" even by some preachers of the Gospel. Controversy or no, the rapture of the Church is coming. The truth is found throughout scripture. The question is, will you miss it because you refuse to look for it and make yourself ready? You must be spiritually fit, prayerfully waiting and watching for this event.

THE SECOND COMING AND THE MILLENNIUM

Many people, especially in the church world today, shy away from the Old Testament. I have heard it said that the Old Testament has been done away with because we are no longer under the law but under grace. The truth is the Old Testament is very much alive and very much real. Let me clue you in on something: Matthew, Mark, Luke and John were all under the law. All four of those gospels were under the law. The whole time Jesus walked on the earth and performed His ministry, was dealing with the Law. The fact is, He came to fulfill those things in Himself. Really, the Church didn't start until the book of Acts. Jesus came to fulfill the Law. The four gospels act as a kind of link between the law and the new covenant.

The Old Testament has a lot of prophecy in it and deals with many things that are very current and very real. Ezekiel 47:1-9 deals with the Millennial Reign:

Afterward he brought me again unto the door of the house; and, behold, waters issued out from under the threshold of the house eastward: for the forefront of the house stood toward the east, and the waters came down from under from the right side of the house, at the south side of the altar.

Then brought he me out of the way of the gate northward, and led me about the way without unto the utter gate by the way that looketh eastward; and, behold, there ran out waters on the right side.

And when the man that had the line in his hand went forth eastward, he measured a thousand cubits, and he brought me through the waters; the waters were to the ankles.

Again he measured a thousand, and brought me through the waters; the waters were to the knees. Again he measured a thousand, and brought me through; the waters were to the loins.

Afterward he measured a thousand; and it was a river that I could not pass over: for the waters were risen, waters to swim in, a river that could not be passed over.

And he said unto me, Son of man, hast thou seen this? Then he brought me, and caused me to return to the brink of the river. Now when I had returned, behold, at the bank of the river were very many trees on the one side and on the other.

Then said he unto me, These waters issue out toward the east country, and go down into the desert, and go into the sea: which being brought forth into the sea, the waters shall be healed. And it shall come to pass, that every thing that liveth, which moveth, whithersoever the rivers shall come, shall live: and there shall be a very great multitude of fish, because these waters shall come thither: for they shall be healed; and every thing shall live whither the river cometh.

The book of Revelation takes us through the first half of the tribulation and then the second half, which could be called the Great

Tribulation. After that time, we come to the time of the one hour judgment found in Revelation 18. Revelation 19 brings us to the point of the second coming of Jesus Christ. Some people say they have a one way ticket to heaven. Let me give you a better understanding—you actually have a round trip ticket. There is going to be a rapture and a calling away of the Church out of this world and we will be in the heavens during the tribulation period in the very presence of Almighty God. It will be during that time that the saints of God will be rewarded and they will be crowned. Then in Revelation 19, we see that we come back with Christ to this earth for what is commonly called the Battle of Armageddon. This is a battle that is described in Revelation 19 that will bring to a close that particular era of time, the seven year tribulation period. We will then move into the last dispensational period of time the Bible speaks about, the Millennial Reign.

There are some things I want to point out about the second coming of Jesus Christ. He will come in the clouds of glory. He will come with the saints who are in heaven with Him. Look at Revelation 19:14:

And the armies which were in heaven followed him upon white horses, clothed in fine linen, white and clean.

That's not angels he's talking about. Look at verses 7 and 8 from the same chapter:

Let us be glad and rejoice, and give honour to him: for the marriage of the Lamb is come, and his wife hath made herself ready. And to her was granted that she should be arrayed in fine linen, clean and white: for the fine linen is the righteousness of saints.

These are the same words in each verse when it speaks of fine linen. If you have a hard time believing that there will be a rapture of the Church before the second coming of Christ and that the saints of God will be in heaven and then will return with Jesus when He comes again, answer one question—How did the saints get up in heaven as accounted for in these verses if there was no rapture? Be assured, there is going to be a rapture of the Church. We will be called out of this earth and we will be in the presence of God. The saints of God will sit down with Christ and we're going to partake of the marriage supper of the Lamb. At that point, we're going to be crowned and blessed of God and rewarded by the hand of God.

At the end of the marriage supper of the Lamb, the invitation will be given to the saints to return to earth with Christ. This is described in Zechariah 14 and Matthew 24. Jesus Christ will come back from heaven down to planet earth. Look at Zechariah 14:4:

And his feet shall stand in that day upon the mount of Olives, which is before Jerusalem on the east, and the mount of Olives shall cleave in the midst thereof toward the east and toward the west, and there shall be a very great valley; and half of the mountain shall remove toward the north, and half of it toward the south.

It is at this point that the anti-Christ and those who took the mark of the beast will be gathered together in time "to make war against Him who sat on the horse and against His army." Look at Revelation 19:11:

And I saw heaven opened, and behold a white horse; and he that sat upon him was called Faithful and True, and in righteousness he doth judge and make war. His eyes were as a flame of fire, and on his head were many crowns; and he had a name written, that no man knew, but he himself. And he was clothed with a vesture dipped in blood: and his name is called The Word of God.

And the armies which were in heaven followed him upon white horses, clothed in fine linen, white and clean. And out of his mouth goeth a sharp sword, that with it he should smite the nations: and he shall rule them with a rod of iron: and he treadeth the winepress of the fierceness and wrath of Almighty God. And he hath on his vesture and on his thigh a name written, KING OF KINGS, AND LORD OF LORDS.

And I saw an angel standing in the sun; and he cried with a loud voice, saying to all the fowls that fly in the midst of heaven, Come and gather yourselves together unto the supper of the great God; that ye may eat the flesh of kings, and the flesh of captains, and the flesh of mighty men, and the flesh of horses, and of them that sit on them, and the flesh of all men, both free and bond, both small and great.

And I saw the beast, and the kings of the earth, and their armies, gathered together to make war against him that sat on the horse, and against his army. And the beast was taken, and with him the false prophet that wrought miracles before him, with which he deceived them that had received the mark of the beast, and them that worshipped his image. These both were cast alive into a lake of fire burning with brimstone.

And the remnant were slain with the sword of him that sat upon the horse, which sword proceeded out of his mouth: and all the fowls were filled with their flesh.

Before we look at Revelation 20 which deals with the Millennial Reign, we need to understand what we have read in chapter 19. God refers to the armies of heaven—that's you and I, the saints of God—and He says that we will be coming back with Him. The saints will be gathered together from every nation in this world. All of those who have received the mark of the beast will be destroyed and killed in the Battle of Armageddon. That means there is going to be some who did not receive the mark of the beast. They will show up in the Millennial Reign.

When Jesus comes back to earth, the brightness of His coming is going to destroy the anti-Christ. The brightness of the second coming of Jesus Christ and the Word of Almighty God will destroy the anti-Christ! The Word of God is the most powerful thing this side of heaven. To see how powerful the Word of God is, look at Revelation 11:15:

And the seventh angel sounded; and there were great voices in heaven, saying, the kingdoms of this world are become the kingdoms of our Lord, and of his Christ; and he shall reign for ever and ever.

Just a word from heaven and the enemy of your soul is stripped of everything that he has. Simply by a Word from Almighty God! What a powerful thing we have when we have the Word of Almighty God!

Look at 2 Thessalonians 2:7-8:

For the mystery of iniquity doth already work: only he who now letteth will let, until he be taken out of the way. And then shall that Wicked be revealed, whom the Lord shall consume with the spirit of his mouth, and shall destroy with the brightness of his coming.

Allow me to explain this a bit. The last phrase of verse 7 declares that something has got to be taken out of the way before the anti-Christ can be revealed. Only then shall that Wicked be revealed. Something has got to leave here before the anti-Christ can be revealed and that something is the Church of the Living God. Some think this is referring to the Holy Ghost. This is incorrect. The Holy Ghost will be here all the way through the tribulation period. He will seal the 144,000. The Holy Ghost will still be calling people to God and there will be people saved. For confirmation of this you need only look to Acts 2:17-21:

And it shall come to pass in the last days, saith God, I will pour out of my Spirit upon all flesh: and your sons and your daughters shall prophesy, and your young men shall see visions, and your old men shall dream dreams: And on my servants and on my handmaidens I will pour out in those days of my Spirit; and they shall prophesy:

And I will shew wonders in heaven above, and signs in the earth beneath; blood, and fire, and vapour of smoke: The sun shall be turned into darkness, and the moon into blood, before the great and notable day of the Lord come:

And it shall come to pass, that whosoever shall call on the name of the Lord shall be saved.

In order to be saved, you have to be convicted and drawn by the Spirit of God. The Bible here describes the sun turning dark, the moon turning to blood, and that during that time it shall come to pass that "whosoever shall call on the name of the Lord shall be saved." Here is our indication that the Spirit is going to still be present.

To accept that scripture is speaking of the Church in 2 Thessalonians 2:7-8, there may be a lingering question *when and where is the Church ever referred to as a "he"?* The Church is referred to as the body of Christ in 1 Corinthians. When the Church is compared to the world, we are always referred to in terms of power and masculinity. When we are compared to Jesus Christ, we are referred to as the bride and the Church. We are spoken of in our frailty when compared to Jesus Christ because He is all powerful. You may not feel powerful and most of the time, we don't act like it, but we are the most powerful entity this side of heaven. The Church of the Living God is holding hell at bay. We need to start acting like the powerhouse that we are by using the Word of God and the strength that God has given us through the Spirit and the Word.

When it goes on to say in the passage from 2 Thessalonians "and then shall that Wicked be revealed," this is the anti-Christ revealed. There is a reason the devil wants to denounce and put down the Church of God. When we're called out of here, there will be nothing here to keep the powers of hell from running rampant.

Returning to Revelation 19, the armies of heaven—which refers to us—will come back with Christ and when we do, we will watch Him fight the final battle. He's going to fight the final battle called the Battle of Armageddon. That closes the tribulation period and opens a brand new time. It opens a time that is referred to in Revelation 20 as the Millennial Reign. Notice in the first seven verses of chapter 20, six times in these verses, 1,000 years is referred to. This period comes after the close of the tribulation period and it is a definite period in time with a start day and an end day. During that time, we will reign with Christ on this earth for 1,000 years.

Why did God make a seven day week? He could have made it a 10 day week, rounded a day off to 25 hours, and we could have gotten more done, but God does nothing just to be doing. Everything He does has a reason and a purpose. From day one to day end, the seven days represents a time in history. There have been 6,000 years from Adam to now. We're coming to the close of 6,000 years. On the 7th day of creation, God rested. The Bible said in 2 Peter 3:8, "But, beloved, be not ignorant of this one thing, that one day is with the Lord as a thousand years, and a thousand years as one day." Each day of time represents 1,000 years of history for us.

In Genesis 1, we have the creation account. Isn't it ironic that on day 1 of the creation, God said "let there be light and there was light," but He didn't make a sun or a moon or a star until day 4? I said earlier that God doesn't do anything just to be doing. Can you understand the darkness that was on the face of this earth? The Bible says God put a firmament in the midst of the waters and He called the firmament heaven. So this earth was covered with water all the way from the crust of the earth up through the clouds. The depth of the darkness you can't comprehend nor can you imagine. There was no sun that couldn shine through that, but God said on day 1, "let there be light," and the crust of this earth began to illuminate with the light of Jesus Christ.

Jesus said many times, "I am the light of the world." Scripture says in John 1:1-5:

In the beginning was the Word, and the Word was with God, and the Word was God. The same was in the beginning with God. All things were made by him; and without him was not any thing made that was made. In him was life; and the life was the light of men. And the light shineth in darkness; and the darkness comprehended it not.

Verse 14 goes on to say, "the Word was made flesh, and dwelt among us, (and we beheld his glory, the glory as of the only begotten of the Father,) full of grace and truth." John is reiterating that there was a light that shone on this globe and lit it up for four days before God ever made a sun or a moon. Why did God put the sun and moon in place on day 4? Isn't it amazing that there were 4,000 years from the time of Adam to the birth of Christ? The first 4,000 years the light was shining to say the Messiah is coming and then He came.

In Genesis 1, it says repeatedly that the evening and the morning were the day. Why did God repeat this in His Word? You and I live from daylight to dark, but God lives from evening to morning. He brings us from darkness into the marvelous light. From the very beginning, In Genesis 1, there is a message about salvation—there is nobody too lost, too deep in sin that the light of God can't shine through.

There will be a Millennial Reign with day one to day end spanning 1,000 years. This Millenial Regin will fit in the slot of the 7th day of rest. It brings to completion life on this planet then we will move into the new heaven and the new earth.

Look at Revelation 20:1-7:

And I saw an angel come down from heaven, having the key of the bottomless pit and a great chain in his hand. And he laid hold on the dragon, that old serpent, which is the Devil, and Satan, and bound him a thousand years, And cast him into the bottomless pit, and shut him up, and set a seal upon him, that he should deceive the nations no more, till the thousand years should be fulfilled: and after that he must be loosed a little season.

And I saw thrones, and they sat upon them, and judgment was given unto them: and I saw the souls of them that were beheaded for the witness of Jesus, and for the word of God, and which had not worshipped the beast, neither his image, neither had received his mark upon their foreheads, or in their hands; and they lived and reigned with Christ a thousand years.

But the rest of the dead lived not again until the thousand years were finished. This is the first resurrection. Blessed and holy is he that hath part in the first resurrection: on such the second death hath no power, but they shall be priests of God and of Christ, and shall reign with him a thousand years. And when the thousand years are expired, Satan shall be loosed out of his prison.

In this passage, the author repeatedly says "1,000 years." There is going to be a period of time that our Lord shall come back to this earth and set a kingdom up on the earth for 1,000 years. God is simply reclaiming everything by His Word and His power.

We read earlier in Ezekiel 47 about the river of God that is going to flow. After the tribulation period, the earth will be in shambles. We know that God can take a life that is in shambles and when He is done with it, it is restored and renewed and worth something. Everything God touches lives. When the Lord sets His kingdom up on this earth, the earth will no longer be in shambles. He is going to heal everything. That old tree that died during the tribulation period—the top is gone, the bark is falling off the sides—when the river touches it, the top comes back and the bark tightens up and there will be leaves all over it because there's life in the river of God. He's going to restore everything. That river will flow down and into the Dead Sea and the river will heal the Dead Sea. When it does, it will become a fisherman's paradise (Ezekiel 47:9-12) during the Millennial Reign.

We will rule and reign with Christ during the Millennial Reign. There's going to be men and women who will walk right out from the tribulation period who did not receive the mark of the beast who will come right out into the Millennial Reign and we will reign with them.

When the devil is released from his prison, he will gather these people together and they will come against the holy city and the camp of the saints. Understand this: God Himself determines who will rule and who will be ruled. For clarification, look at 1 Corinthians 6:2-3:

> *Do ye not know that the saints shall judge the world? and if the world shall be judged by you, are ye unworthy to judge the smallest matters? Know ye not that we shall judge angels? how much more things that pertain to this life?*

That's got to be talking about the Millennial Reign because the saints aren't going to rule this earth nor will we rule angels until the

Millennial Reign. How you live your life right here is the determining factor of how you rule and reign with Him on the other side.

I hear so many church people say it's nobody's business how they live their lives. Yes it is! When you come to the house of God and hang your shingle out that you're a born again believer, you must be directed and taught by those God has put in place to teach because God is training you to rule with Him in the Millennial Reign. This includes teaching in how you treat your family, how you perform your job, how you act in church, and how faithful you are to God. You must be taught things of God in all areas to prepare you to reign.

Look at Colossians 3:18-24:

Wives, submit yourselves unto your own husbands, as it is fit in the Lord. Husbands, love your wives, and be not bitter against them. Children, obey your parents in all things: for this is well pleasing unto the Lord. Fathers, provoke not your children to anger, lest they be discouraged. Servants, obey in all things your masters according to the flesh; not with eyeservice, as menpleasers; but in singleness of heart, fearing God; And whatsoever ye do, do it heartily, as to the Lord, and not unto men; knowing that of the Lord ye shall receive the reward of the inheritance: for ye serve the Lord Christ.

That is some rich stuff. All of these things are important—our behavior at home, what kind of wife, husband, child and father you are and how you do your job—these are the determining factors as to what kind of inheritance reward we will receive.

When are we going to get the inheritance reward? 2 Timothy 4:8 tells us, "Henceforth there is laid up for me a crown of righteousness, which the Lord, the righteous judge, shall give me at that day: and not to me only, but unto all them also that love his appearing." We don't think our performance here on earth is important. To some, even considering our performance is "works". Let me tell you, you can't get saved by works, but after you are saved, your works are very important to God. The Bible says we will have to give an account for the works that we do. We do not earn our salvation, it is gift of God, but after you are saved, your performance toward God and your family is directly related to how you will rule and reign with Him. That may not mean much to you right now, but when you're living in eternity and you're 2,600 years old and you're still a flunky, your may wish you had behaved differently right now. We are eternal beings. We are going to live forever somewhere.

When God made man, He only made one man from the dust of the ground. Genesis 2:7 tells us this and it says that "He breathed into his nostrils the breath of life and he became a living soul." The Hebrew word picture is this, that God cast His shadow on the ground and with His finger He traced His shadow out and with His breath He breathed into that shadow and man just peeled right out of the ground. The breath of God is not your soul, it is the glue that holds your soul and spirit into your body. When God calls His breath home, there will be nothing to keep you together. At the rapture, your inner man is going to leave this body and you will get a brand new body.

Genesis 1:26-27 tell us that Adam was made in the image of God, but Adam and Eve sinned, they failed God. 1 Timothy 2:14 tells us that "Adam was not deceived but Eve, being deceived, was in transgression." Adam was not deceived, he walked in willfully. Eve was deceived by the enemy and she partook of the forbidden fruit. Adam willfully sinned so he and Eve would not be eternally separated. The last Adam—Christ—willfully becomes sin for us so that we would not be eternally separated from Him.

As Adam and Eve sinned, something changed. In Genesis 5:3, it says that "Adam was 130 years old and he begot a son after his likeness or image and he called his name Seth." You see, we never lost the image of God, but we did lose the likeness of God. This helps explain why Jesus says we must be born again. The image of God is his physical qualities—scripture speaks about the eyes of God, the hands of God, etc. This is the image of God which we maintain, but we lost the likeness of God when man sinned. We are to strive to get that back—to be like Him. Every day, let us progress into the likeness of our Lord and Savior Jesus Christ. This can be achieved. It's not out of reach—this is the purpose and the plan of God. How we live this life is the determining factor of how we rule and reign with Him.

Ephesians 5:25 tells husbands to love their wives as Christ loved the Church and gave Himself up for the Church. It makes a difference how you love your family. how you act, how you treat your neighbor; how you work on the job and how your worship. This is the determining factor of how you rule and reign with the Lord. There's going to be little old ladies who come before the Lord in the Millennial Reign who never held a position in the church, the community didn't know them, but they raised a house full of kids and they worked in the community and they baked pies and cakes and they were at the door greeting and they were faithful. Christ will say to them, "I'll put you over 10,000. Go down there by the sea and take care of that 10,000." Likewise, there will be preachers who will come before the Lord and He will say, "The whole time I called you, you bellyached and griped. There's 10 people, let's see if you can handle them and if you can't, I'm gonna give them to that little old lady who has 10,000. 10 more won't hurt her at all!" How you act in this life is a determining factor of how you're going to rule and reign with Christ during the Millenial Reign.

After we have been there with Him ruling and reigning for 1,000 years, at the end of that time, Satan will be loosed out of his prison. There will be natural people who will appear during that time. It amazes me to think that there will be people who will live under the earthly reign of Jesus Christ and still rebel against Him. It's amazing how the enemy has influence on the human mind. We can be deceived, we can be led astray. Scripture warns us to take heed lest we fall—don't ever have a high and haughty spirit. Always stay humble and keep the Word of God in your heart because the Word of God provides the stability and standard God set for us.

At the end of the Millenial Reign, Satan is loosed out of his prison and he goes to the four corners of the earth. Look at Revelation 20:8-9:

> *And shall go out to deceive the nations which are in the four quarters of the earth, Gog, and Magog, to gather them together to battle: the number of whom is as the sand of the sea. And they went up on the breadth of the earth, and compassed the camp of the saints about, and the beloved city: and fire came down from God out of heaven, and devoured them.*

These people who gather with Satan for battle would have seen, known, and experienced the living Lord and would have known what had happened in the past and yet they are still deceived by the enemy of our soul to join with him in one final battle. These people will come from everywhere. Gog is not the name of a person but a place, Ezekiel 38 and 39 mention the land of Gog and Magog. After 1,000 years Millennial Reign, Gog and Magog rise again. Satan gathers his army and they pass the camp of the saints. When they do, God rains fire down out of heaven and consumes them.

Satan, who deceived them, is then cast in the lake of fire and brimstone where the beast and false prophets are and where they shall be tormented day and night forever and ever (Revelation 20:10). This is the last of Lucifer. No more deceiving, no more trials or tests or temptations. It's over at that point. Sometimes I have to re-read Revelation 20:10 over and over to remind myself that one day, every demon in hell, including Lucifer himself, will be cast into the lake of fire. You may wonder if the lake of fire is forever and if human souls will go there. Remember, the anti-Christ and the false prophets are human souls. They are cast into the lake of fire. There is an eternal damnation for the soul of mankind that rejects God Almighty.

The word "sanctification" has been swept aside all too often. We, the Church, need to be sanctified. We need to live clean, holy, and righteous before God. We need to be all that God intends for us to be as we put ourselves in the hands of the Lord Jesus Christ. The way we live our life is important as it will determine how we rule and reign with Christ.

WHITE THRONE JUDGMENT AND HELL

The topics of the White Throne Judgment and hell are very important. I have a personal story that will illustrate this importance. Several years ago, I preached a message on hell. There was a fellow in the church who purchased a cassette tape of the sermon after the service. This man was a bus driver who drove the senior basketball team around. One night, he was driving the team back from a game. They had lost that night and he knew the boys on the team were tender. He put the tape of the sermon into the player on the bus and played that message on hell. Over 30 of the boys on that team gave their heart and lives to Jesus Christ that night.

It is important that we understand there is an eternity and it is very real. God speaks of this often in His Word. It is important for us to know what the Word of God says.

There is much misconception about what heaven will be like. So many believe and teach that in heaven, we will just bow down and worship for millions of years. When I heard people saying these things, I thought *God help me!* I knew I would be in serious trouble. Growing up, I got a whipping every Sunday night after church. You could count on that because I was a hyper child. The thought of bowing in worship for millions of years was not appealing. But heaven is more than that. We will assume a new life there.

To get a better understanding of the White Throne Judgment and hell, let's begin our study in Revelation 20:11-15:

> *And I saw a great white throne, and him that sat on it, from whose face the earth and the heaven fled away; and there was found no place for them. And I saw the dead, small and great, stand before God; and the books were opened: and another book was opened, which is the book of life: and the dead were judged out of those things which were written in the books, according to their works. And the sea gave up the dead which were in it; and death and hell delivered up the dead which were in them: and they were judged every man according to their works. And death and hell were cast into the lake of fire. This is the second death. And whosoever was not found written in the book of life was cast into the lake of fire.*

At the end of the Millennial Reign, after those 1,000 years, we will go immediately into the White Throne Judgment. So many people comment that when they stand before the White Throne Judgment, they hope everything is clear in their life. You'd better hope you don't stand before the White Throne Judgment! The White Throne Judgment is for the wicked dead. At this point, the saints of God have already been judged and rewarded and crowned. Look at Revelation 11:15-18:

And the seventh angel sounded; and there were great voices in heaven, saying, The kingdoms of this world are become the kingdoms of our Lord, and of his Christ; and he shall reign for ever and ever. And the four and twenty elders, which sat before God on their seats, fell upon their faces, and worshipped God, saying, We give thee thanks, O LORD God Almighty, which art, and wast, and art to come; because thou hast taken to thee thy great power, and hast reigned.

And the nations were angry, and thy wrath is come, and the time of the dead, that they should be judged, and that thou shouldest give reward unto thy servants the prophets, and to the saints, and them that fear thy name, small and great; and shouldest destroy them which destroy the earth.

Verse 18 of this passage gives indication that the saints of God are going to be rewarded during the time from the time of the rapture of the Church until the second coming. Those taken in the rapture of the Church will not be surprised. Those who are raptured will have been looking for that event and they would have made themselves ready.

You see in this passage there are three groups of people rewarded. The first group includes the servants and the prophets. They are first because they are ministers before God and they serve the people as well, so God rewards them first. The second group includes saints and them that fear the name of the Lord, both small and great. There are no "Big I's and little you's" in the sight of God. You are blessed and rewarded according to what you have done for God in your life. We make it to the eternal kingdom of God through and by the blood of Jesus Christ alone, but the reward of serving and reigning with Christ during the Millennial Reign is given according to your righteous acts when you were on earth.

The White Throne Judgment takes place for the wicked dead. This is also called the second resurrection. The first resurrection is for the dead in Christ and the raptured saints—those that have come through the era of grace. The first resurrection is spoken about in Revelation 20:5 where it is says that blessed is he who takes part in the first resurrection. By the time you reach the events spoken of in Revelation 20:11, the Dispensation of Grace has already passed. Grace is over, judgment has come. Today He's your Savior, tomorrow, He may be your judge.

Throughout time, God has dealt with man in various ways according to the covenant in place at that time. For example, during the time of man's innocence, after God had placed him in the garden but before he had sinned, God walked with man in the cool of the day and enjoyed uninterrupted fellowship with him. After man sinned, God dealt with him differently.

During the first 6 chapters of Genesis, God was showing Adam that He was bringing mankind back from the fall into the saving knowledge of the Lord. When Adam and Eve came out of hiding after they had sinned, they were clothed with fig leaves and God told them that wouldn't cut it. They could not cover their own sin, so God performed the first sacrifice when He sacrificed animals and took their skins—the Jews say it was the skins of lambs—to cover the nakedness of mankind. This was the first sacrifice.

Do you realize that Cain and Abel were twins (Genesis 4:1-2)? This is important because it means that both of them were raised at the same time under the same teaching and knew about the blood covenant. When Cain and Abel brought their sacrifices before God, they had both had the same teaching concerning the necessity of blood sacrifice. But Cain brought his sacrifice from what he harvested from the earth. Why was this not acceptable? Because God had cursed the earth so He rejected Cain's sacrifice. In the New Testament, John 10 tells us that "if you try to come to heaven through any other way but Christ, you are the same as a thief and a robber." That has been the personality of God from Genesis through Revelation. You must be born again through and by the blood of Jesus Christ.

It was God Who initiated the blood covenant when he clothed Adam and Eve after they sinned. When Adam and Eve sinned and their eyes were opened, they realized they were naked. Previously, they were clothed in righteousness. When they sinned, they lost their righteousness before God. When they sinned, their eyes were opened and they knew that they were naked. Do you realize that from that time on, it has been the heartbeat of God to clothe you in His righteousness? In the end, you will be reclothed in righteousness. Look at Revelation 19:7-8:

> *Let us be glad and rejoice, and give honour to him: for the marriage of the Lamb is come, and his wife hath made herself ready. And to her was granted that she should be arrayed in fine linen, clean and white: for the fine linen is the righteousness of saints.*

The fine linen mentioned here is the righteous of the saints. That's the uniform that we'll wear when we get to heaven. It is the righteousness of God.

The first resurrection is for the righteous dead and the raptured saints. The second resurrection is for the wicked dead as they enter the White Throne Judgment. John tells us in Revelation 20:12 "that he saw the dead, small and great, standing before God. Then the books were opened." One of these books is the Bible. The Bible is a testament of God's will and direction for our life. We must become good stewards of the Word of God. Don't think that if you don't read the Bible, you will be excused from responsibility. You have been given the Word of God and you are responsible for knowing what it says. We will give an account for what we have done with the Word of God, that is why the Bible is opened.

Another book that is opened is the Book of Life. The Book of Life is opened to show that there are no sinners' names listed in the Book of Life. God opens this book to show the wicked that their names are not there to prove that He is a just God.

After the books are opened, the dead are judged out of those things that are written according to the lives they lived. Look at 2 Corinthians 5:10:

For we must all appear before the judgment seat of Christ; that every one may receive the things done in his body, according to that he hath done, whether it be good or bad.

That applies to the saints and the wicked dead as well—we are all going to give account for what we have done. Aren't you glad that the old account was settled long ago through and by the blood of Jesus Christ?

Understand that there is a difference between hell and the lake of fire. These are two separate places. Revelation 20:14 tells us "that death and hell are cast into the lake of fire." There is a difference between hell and the lake of fire. Hell is a place where the wicked dead go to at death. After they stand before God on the White Throne Judgment day and are judged, they will be cast into the lake of fire.

Perhaps this illustration will help you understand. After a person commits a crime, a police officer comes to arrest them, handcuffs them and takes them to the jail to be held until their court date comes. This holding cell operates the same way as hell. Hell holds the soul of the wicked dead until judgment day. It is important that you understand this. There is a literal hell that houses the souls of mankind who have rejected God. When you leave this life without Jesus Christ in your heart and life, your soul is sent to the place of the damned. There have been people there for hundreds and thousands of years who are waiting for the White Throne Judgment.

Revelation 20 says that death and hell gave up their dead that were in them and they were judged according to their work. When the soul of man dies, there are only two places where that soul can go: hell or heaven. The soul of man who is wicked dead leaves here and goes into hell, but the soul of the righteous that dies goes into the presence of God. In 2 Corinthians 5:8, Paul says "that to be absent from the body is to be present with the Lord." So we see that the saints of God are in the presence of God until the rapture of the Church.

Revelation 20 also says that before the White Throne Judgment, the sea gave up the dead that were in them. What is that talking about? This is talking about the sea giving up the bodies, the physical bodies, of those in it. The physical body and the soul will be reunited at the White Throne Judgment. The next phrase in this passage says that death will release the soul that's in hell. That explains what scripture means when it talks about the second death. This is something that confuses many people. When the soul is united with the body in resurrection, they will stand before God and give an account for the life that they have lived. It makes no difference who they were—kings, queens, paupers—it makes no difference, they are going to stand before God. Their old body will be renewed. In Matthew 10:28, Jesus said don't fear man who can destroy the body, instead fear God Who can destroy both soul and body. At death, the soul goes to hell and the body goes to the grave. When they have been reunited and stand before God, they will give an account for what they have done in this life. The books are going to be opened and they will be judged and then death and hell will be cast into the lake of fire.

It is said in Corinthians that death is the last enemy that is going to be destroyed. Why is that? Because when we enter into the eternal kingdom, there will be no death at all. It is strange for us to imagine no death, but the fact is, you are an eternal creature. You're going to live forever—not 50 or 70 or 90 years or 500 years—and you won't need a walker and you'll never shuffle.

Jesus makes the statement that if your eyes are causing you to go to hell, you would be much better off to pluck them out and go through this world blind than allow your eyes to send you to hell. He is stressing the importance of escaping the place of the damned where people go and are separated from family and God and then spend eternity in the lake of fire. We don't know how hot the lake of fire is. The Bible refers to it as a lake of fire and brimstone. We do know that one ingredient of brimstone is sulfur. Sulfur has the ability to heat up to 465 degrees Fahrenheit. Now that's hot! To put that in perspective, water boils at 212 degrees Fahrenheit. Your body temperature is normally 98.6 degrees Fahrenheit. If you get a 102 or 103 degree fever, that's dangerously high. 105 degrees can send you into convulsions. We're talking about 465 degrees Fahrenheit and you can't die. You're there forever and ever because you chose to be separated from God. You chose.

There are people today who don't realize they're not saved. They believe that because they live in America, they're Christians and because they gave $10,000 to their favorite charity they're *really* Christians. But when the book of Life is opened they will find that their names are not there. God is a fair and just God and He will show them that their names are not included in the Book of Life. Can you imagine what a prayer meeting is going to take place that day at the White Throne Judgment? But it will be too late. There won't be anyone saved at the White Throne Judgment, the time of grace is over. The Bible says in Hebrews 9:27 "that it is appointed a man once to die and then the judgment." There are deceivers in this world today who would lead people to believe that when they die, they still have a chance to get right with God. The truth is, if you leave this world lost without God, that's how you're going to end up in eternity—lost without God.

The Bible said you *must* be born again. You've got to come through and by the blood of the Lord Jesus Christ alone. There is so much false teaching today saying that it doesn't make any difference, we're all just trying to get to the same place and just taking different routes to get there. The truth is, there is only one heaven, the one where Jesus reigns, and you must go through Him to get there. It's just that simple. There are no gray areas. You must be born again. Acts 4:12 makes this clear when it says "there is no other name under heaven by which man can be saved." Our salvation has got to come through and by Jesus Christ, our Lord and Savior.

In the lake of fire, there are degrees of punishment. In Matthew 10:15, Jesus says these words:

Verily I say unto you, It shall be more tolerable for the land of Sodom and Gomorrha in the day of judgment, than for that city.

He goes further in Matthew 11:22 to say:

But I say unto you, It shall be more tolerable for Tyre and Sidon at the day of judgment, than for you.

And in Matthew 23:14, Jesus says:

Woe unto you, scribes and Pharisees, hypocrites! for ye devour widows' houses, and for a pretence make long prayer: therefore ye shall receive the greater damnation.

All of these statements of Christ reflect the fact that there are degrees of punishment in the lake of fire. For those who have rejected Jesus Christ as Savior of this world, there are degrees of punishment.

Death always causes separation. It separates the body from the soul. You're made of three parts: spirit, soul, and body and in that order. Spirit and soul are eternal, which means that two parts of you are eternal and only one part is natural. You are an eternal creature. You will live somewhere in eternity and where that place is, will be up to you. Jesus did all the groundwork to provide you with the option of living with Him for eternity. He died on the cross of Calvary to make a way for you, but you must make the choice to accept the salvation He offers. You decide whether you want to go to hell or heaven. If you want to go to heaven, you follow the path that Jesus Christ leads you down. If you want to go to hell, all you have to do is reject Jesus Christ and live life as you want to and you will end up in hell—lost without God.

Some people will say He's not that kind of God, He won't send anybody to hell. I will agree to that to a point, He doesn't send you to hell, you send yourself. God made a way of escape and if you choose not to go that way, you have made your choice to be lost without God. He has made a path to salvation, but it's up to you and me to choose that path. He's not sending anybody's soul to hell. In fact, He said "it's not His will that any should perish but that all come to repentance." God is more willing to save people than people are to be saved. In fact, we're more willing to send people to hell than God is. God is merciful. He's doing everything He can to bring mankind back to Himself to bring them to the promise of heaven and the glory of His love. But we must make a choice.

Let me talk about hell for a moment. Where is hell located? I believe scripture confirms that hell is in the center of the earth. Look at Matthew 12:40:

For as Jonas was three days and three nights in the whale's belly; so shall the Son of an be three days and three nights in the heart of the earth.

Do you realize that when Jesus died on the cross of Calvary, said "It is finished," and closed His eyes in death, when they took Him from the cross, wrapped Him in cloth and laid Him in the tomb and three days later He rose from the dead – during those three days, He descended into the heart of the earth. Ephesians 4:8-9 confirms this. He went down in the regions of the damned to show you and I that He paid the eternal price for our soul. Look at Acts 2:31 where Peter is speaking of Christ:

He seeing this before spake of the resurrection of Christ, that his soul was not left in hell, neither his flesh did see corruption.

You can't be left somewhere you've never been. During those three days when the body of Jesus lay in the tomb, He went into the regions of the damned and tasted the flames of hell so we wouldn't have to go. But hell couldn't hold Him because He had not sinned. He triumphed over death, hell, and the grave. He became victorious for us and conquered death, hell, and the grave. We were headed for hell and we deserved hell because we sinned, but Jesus tasted the flames of hell and then walked out of there, triumphant, bringing victory for you and I through His Name! Through His Name, He saved us and redeemed us.

Hell is a holding place for the departed souls of man who are not saved and are waiting for the judgment day. Men don't like to speak of this holding place of the soul, yet they use it as a byword everyday.

It should never be used as a byword because it is the place of damnation for the soul of the wicked dead, those who do not know Jesus Christ as Savior.

Many people have described hell in different ways. On July 4, 1943, Hamburg, Germany was bombed during World War 2 by the allies in an attempt to defeat Hitler and his armies. 750 bombers loaded with bombs left out from airports and ships all over Europe. They all converged on Hamburg and dropped their bombs. Many people ran to bomb shelters, but none survived. The heat was intense. It was reported that flames leapt three miles into the sky, balls of fire shot eight miles into the air. There was a vacuum wind of 150 mph created from this inferno. The allies lost more planes due to that wind than any enemy ever shot down. It was devastating. After it was all over with, troops went into the city and found scratch marks and blood trails in sidewalks. They found one man in his late 20's who had been on the outskirts of the city and had witnessed the entire ordeal. His hair had turned entirely white. The only words he spoke from that time until the day he died were, "It was hell on earth." He was literally driven out of his mind.

I've thought about that so many times. This bombing only a short period, but hell is a place you do not escape until the White Throne Judgment. That is why God tells us it is important for you and me to reach the lost and the dying. We think of hell only in passing without really realizing how intense and terrible it is that someone would die and actually go to hell. Hell is described in the book of Matthew as being a place of weeping, wailing, and gnashing of teeth. It's like an insane asylum and people have been there for multiplied years without any hope. All they have to look toward is the White Throne Judgment when hell releases its dead and they are then on their way to the lake of fire. What a tragedy. How excruciating this must be on the minds of those there facing this reality.

In Luke 16, we see the story of the rich man and Lazarus. Some say this is a parable, but I believe it to be a true account because the Word of God says, "There *was* a certain rich man." I believe this story exists as a truth and fact. The story says the rich man died and lifted up his eyes from hell where he was in torment from the flames. The story says that Lazarus died and was carried by angels into Abraham's bosom. A reader might be confused because it says that the rich man could look across the great gulf (Luke 16:26). When he saw Lazarus, he cried out. He begged Abraham to send Lazarus to dip his finger into cool water to sooth his tongue as he was tormented in the flames. Abraham tells the rich man that they cannot cross the gulf—the rich man cannot come to them and they cannot go to him.

The soul of man that is wicked dead is in hell. There have been souls there for centuries of time. Cain is there. King Saul is there. They are waiting with the only hope ahead the window of time when they escape hell for the White Throne Judgment just before they are cast into the lake of fire.

But for those still living, God's mercy is still offered now. His mercy endures forever to those still living, but those who have died without accepting God's merciful gift of salvation are in the flames of hell suffering torment. Judas Iscariot is there in hell. In Matthew 10:1-4, it tells us that Jesus empowered His disciples and among the listing of those disciples, you will find the name of Judas Iscariot. He was empowered to cast out devils and heal the sick. In Acts 1, Peter says of Judas that he was one of them and even partook of the ministry. Some will say that Judas was the devil or demon possessed. That's not what the Bible says. In John 13:27, we are told that after the sop, Satan entered into Judas. Judas was toying with some thoughts and was badly oppressed, but he didn't become demon possessed until the Last Supper when he was sitting with Jesus and the disciples. Jesus confirmed that whoever dipped the sop with Him was the one who would betray Him. After Judas dipped the sop, then Satan entered into him. Because Judas never repented of his sins, he is now in hell. How many times must Judas have thought through the years he has been in hell, *I could have had a foundation in the New Jerusalem named after me! I took part in the ministry! I was there when Lazarus came forth from the dead and I saw Him heal the sick! What was I thinking?!* There are people in hell with these same thoughts of regret today. Real people that you rub shoulders with every day are headed to hell without God and what are we doing about it?

The problem is that we have no concept of what hell is truly like. The Bible says that there, the worm does not die. There are worms in hell that gnaw on the soul of mankind and yet man cannot die. Men are begging for death in hell, but they cannot die. They are eternal creatures. The soul and spirit do not die. What you need is the blood of Jesus Christ in your heart to keep you from winding up in hell without God. Hell wasn't made for mankind. It was made for the devil and his angels, but because of man's rejection of Christ, hell has engulfed the souls of millions throughout the course of time.

I remember when I pastored in Pine Bluff, you could look down Turner Street from our church. I received a note from someone who told me that there was a man who lived on Turner Street who had, at one time, attended church but now was not and he now had terminal cancer. They asked if I would please go visit this man. Of course, I agreed to do so. I took another man from the church with me to make the visit. When we walked in the sick man's bedroom, it was obvious that cancer was devouring him. He was skin and bones. I walked over by the bedside and took his hand as I began to talk to him about the goodness and greatness of God. Tears streamed down this man's face and I began thinking in my mind that he surely would be receptive to our message. I couldn't wait to pray. I knew he was ready—that he would give his heart and mind to Christ and he could go into eternity redeemed and right with God.

I continued talking and then came down to the point where I said to him, "Sir, would you like to turn your life over to Jesus and make Him Lord and Savior of your life?" Immediately he dropped my hand, dried his tears and with a stern look on his face he said, "I have made it this far without Him. I will make it the rest of the way." I felt the Spirit of God leave the room that day. I begged that man to reconsider.

The next day I was in the church office and I heard the sirens from the ambulance coming down the street. I could tell that the ambulance was turning down Turner Street and I ran from the church. I was standing by the telephone pole at the edge of the church property and watched as the ambulance backed up to the man's house where I had been just the day before. The emergency personnel loaded the man up, but he never made it to the hospital.

He went into eternity without God. If there was some way I could step into hell today, I wouldn't have to ask him if he wanted to know Jesus. There's no telling who he would run over to get to me.

In the torments of hell, the drug addict never loses the craving for drugs, the alcoholic never loses the craving for alcohol. The wicked damned are there without God, lost without the Lord. As you read this and the minutes have ticked away, thousands of souls have plunged into hell without God. You'll lay down tonight in your bed to go to sleep and hell may never cross your mind, but hell is very real and it's engulfing the souls of mankind. When you have a family member leave this world and you are not sure whether or not they were right with God, then hell will become more real to you.

Before my father gave his heart and life to the Lord, he was a gambler. That's how he made his living. My grandfather signed papers for him to gamble in the State of Missouri before my father was ever of age. My father ran with a group of young men. He was not raised in church. My grandparents were not church people. My father knew nothing about God, nothing about church, but one night, all of his friends went by the house of one of his buddies and there was an elderly babysitter taking care of one of the younger siblings of my dad's friend. As all my dad's friends walked into the house that night before they were to go out to gamble, this lady sat in a rocking chair and said to the boys, "Boys, I'm praying for you and I hope that you don't wind up in hell without God."

Somehow, that stuck in my father's heart and he wanted to know more about hell. He went to the local church to find out more about hell. The pastor of the church preached on hell and my father went to an altar of prayer and gave his heart and life to Jesus Christ. The first thing he did when he got saved was got a job shoveling coal.

He had been saved for 3 or 4 months and one day, one of his friends came by to visit. He said to my dad, "Ikey, I heard that you got religion." Dad said, "If that's what you want to call it. I go to First Assembly of God Church with Brother Billy Campbell." Dad's friend said he knew the church because his wife and children went to church there. My dad didn't even know his friend was married.

Dad's friend said that his oldest son was always talking to him about coming to church with them. He said he had promised his family that he was going to come, that he was going to straighten up. Dad offered to pray with his friend right there, but his friend declined to do so, saying that he had a party planned. "Would you like to go to one more party and have a good time once more for old times' sake?" he asked my dad. Dad declined and said that he wouldn't go because he was now free from that old life, but he offered again to pray with his friend.

"No thanks, but look for me. I'm coming to church and I'm going to sit with my wife and my family," replied his friend. That afternoon, Dad's friend who had been drinking all day, crossed over the center line into the path of a big truck and went into eternity without God.

When they had his funeral in the church, only a handful of people showed up. There weren't many friends. The most tragic part was the family. The church had to help the family with food and clothes because Dad's friend had gambled and drank away all his income. That day at the funeral service, when they walked by to look for the final time into the face of that husband and father, the oldest boy looked down at his father and with tears streaming down his face, he said, "Daddy, I loved you with everything I've got. I loved you. With all of your faults, I loved you. But where he has now gone, I don't intend to go and now, we are forever separated."

In Revelation 21:4, we see these words:

And God shall wipe away all tears from their eyes; and there shall be no more death, neither sorrow, nor crying, neither shall there be any more pain: for the former things are passed away.

May this ring in your heart until something changes in your life. When you stand before God and you had family that didn't make it, the instant that God takes His big hand and wipes the tears from your eyes, you will forget that they ever existed. But while they are in the regions of the damned, they will never forget Momma's smile, Daddy's touch. They will never forget the pleading and the crying. They'll never forget the sacrifices that were made for them. There will be teenagers who will make it to heaven without Mom or Dad. There will be kids who make it to heaven without their parents. Standing that day before God, as He begins to wipe the tears away from eyes, you forget your loss because heaven is not a place of torment. The former will not be remembered as He wipes the tears away. But those in the place of eternal torment will never forget. They will never forget the services they sat through when God spoke to their hearts and they said, "Not today, not now."

A New Heaven and a New Earth

As we talk about the new heaven and the new earth, we talk about the end of the human race and the beginning of the new. We talk about our new bodies, what we're going to be like, what we're going to do, and what heaven will be like. Let's begin our discussion of the new heaven and the new earth by looking at Matthew 19:27-30:

Then answered Peter and said unto him, Behold, we have forsaken all, and followed thee; what shall we have therefore?

And Jesus said unto them, Verily I say unto you, That ye which have followed me, in the regeneration when the Son of man shall sit in the throne of his glory, ye also shall sit upon twelve thrones, judging the twelve tribes of Israel. And every one that hath forsaken houses, or brethren, or sisters, or father, or mother, or wife, or children, or lands, for my name's sake, shall receive an hundredfold, and shall inherit everlasting life. But many that are first shall be last; and the last shall be first.

This portion of scripture comes just after the account of the rich young ruler. The rich young ruler came to Jesus and asked, "What must I do to have this experience of everlasting life?" Jesus knew all the details about this young man—where he was coming from, what he meant by his question, and where he was headed. Knowing all of this, our Lord does everything possible to teach us. He asks the young man if he has kept the 10 Commandments. The ruler replies, yes, he has kept them from his youth. Jesus tells him that there is just one thing he is lacking—he must sell everything he has, give to the poor, take up his cross and follow Jesus.

The Lord was not trying to make this man a pauper who would live on the streets. He was out to remove the rich young ruler's god. Scripture tells us that the rich young ruler left sorrowfully.

There were some disciples standing there and Peter, who is so much like many of us—a little mouthy and he usually spoke before thinking—said to Jesus (and I'm paraphrasing), "Lord, we have forsaken everything—what are we gonna get out of this thing? What's in it for me?" Jesus answers him with an eternal explanation to his question. In verse 28, Jesus said that those who had followed Him when He walked the earth would sit upon 12 thrones, judging the 12 tribes of Israel. Jesus is saying this to the 12 disciples. Then in verse 29, He speaks to the rest of us when He says for all those who have "forsaken houses, or brethren, or sisters, or father, or mother, or wife, or children, or lands, for my name's sake, shall receive an hundredfold, and shall inherit everlasting life." We know that these comments refer to the end of time because that's when everlasting life kicks in. You and I do not live in everlasting life right now. This body's going to come to a close, but our inner man, our eternal being, is everlasting and when you dedicate yourself to Jesus Christ, you have the promise of everlasting life and living with Him.

The word "forsake" in this passage does not mean abandon. It does not mean you just walk off and leave these things. It means loss—those who have lost these things for the sake of Christ will receive an hundredfold and inherit everlasting life.

Peter saw what had happened in the exchange between Jesus and the rich young ruler and he took advantage of the situation. He saw the rich young ruler as a man who had never been behind on a payment. He had plenty. He had everything together and he had a future. He had everything Peter did not have because he had given it up to follow Christ and now Peter wanted to know what he was going to get out of following Jesus. What was in it for him?

There have been very discouraging times in my life, and I'm sure in yours also, when you've sat down and wondered if this thing of following Christ was all it was made out to be. I've wondered, when this life is over, is it going to be as wonderful as God has declared? Let me tell you with certainty, it will be greater than you've ever dreamed and more wonderful than you can imagine. Heaven is worth sacrificing for. It's worth doing without now. It's worth taking criticism now. Heaven is real and God has prepared it for those who are living for Him.

Heaven is the place Jesus spoke of in John 14:1-6:

Let not your heart be troubled: ye believe in God, believe also in me. In my Father's house are many mansions: if it were not so, I would have told you. I go to prepare a place for you. And if I go and prepare a place for you, I will come again, and receive you unto myself; that where I am, there ye may be also. And whither I go ye know, and the way ye know.

Thomas saith unto him, Lord, we know not whither thou goest; and how can we know the way?

Jesus saith unto him, I am the way, the truth, and the life: no man cometh unto the Father, but by me.

Note in verse 2, Jesus says, "I go to prepare a place for you." This gives us indication that possibly the New Jerusalem had not even been built at that time. Then he says, "...that where I am, there ye may be also."

John continues the description of heaven in Revelation 21:1-2:

And I saw a new heaven and a new earth: for the first heaven and the first earth were passed away; and there was no more sea.

And I John saw the holy city, new Jerusalem, coming down from God out of heaven, prepared as a bride adorned for her husband.

Three things are mentioned here in verses 1 and 2 that John saw: a new heaven, a new earth, and a New Jerusalem. He goes on to describe these things in his vision. He says he was called up there to see all of this. As John writes, we know this a new thing that no one has seen before, except perhaps the Apostle Paul. Note these words of Paul recorded in 2 Corinthians 12:2:

I knew a man in Christ above fourteen years ago, (whether in the body, I cannot tell; or whether out of the body, I

*cannot tell: God knoweth;) such an one caught up to the
third heaven.*

Paul goes on to describe what he saw, though he says they are so
wonderful, he can barely even write about them. It is evident from
this passage that the Apostle Paul and John may have seen the same
things. What you note from each account, however, is that there are
three heavens mentioned to us in the Word of God.

The first heaven is the one you see with the natural eye. This is
where the rain comes from. It includes the clouds in the sky. The
second heaven is the one it takes a telescope to see—space. You can
see Pluto, Neptune, Saturn, Jupiter, Mars and the rest. You can see
these with a telescope. This is the second heaven.

Above both of these, there is the third heaven. This is where God
lives and reigns. This is where the soul of mankind goes as it awaits
the returning of Jesus Christ and the rapture of the Church. This
third heaven is what we will be dealing with in this writing. We will
also talk about the new earth.

There are some good scriptures detailing what will be done with
this earth. Will it be done away with or renovated by fire? It has
been renovated one time by water during Noah's time. The second
time, it will be renovated by fire. In Genesis 49:26, it talks about
everlasting hills on this earth. Psalm 78:69 says the earth is established forever. Psalm 104:5 says the foundation of the earth will not
be removed forever. These and other scriptures verify that God has
established the earth forever. But it will be renovated by fire as
changes are made on this earth.

John says in his writing that he saw no more sea (Revelation 21:1). Right now, two-thirds of earth is covered with water. The new earth John saw was a great land mass. The only water that is mentioned in scripture on this new earth is the river of God and lakes and streams. There will be no more sea, only a huge land mass as God has determined.

This globe that we live on currently has seven land masses, seven continents. But in Genesis 10:25, see that in the days of Peleg was the earth divided. Geologists agree there is a possibility that at one time, this earth was just one large mass of land. Something catastrophic happened that divided the mass. In Genesis 11, we see the story of when Nimrod and the others built the Tower of Babel. Nimrod was the architect of the Tower of Babel. He and the people desired to build a tower so they would not be scattered over the face of the earth. Understand, God made the earth the way He wanted it to be and placed man here, but man did what he desired and discarded God's plans. After this, the earth was cursed.

After seeing the new earth which had no more sea, in Revelation 21:16 John then saw the New Jerusalem coming down out of heaven. When you mention heaven, people get starry eyed as they think of streets of gold, gates of pearl, walls of jasper—but that's not heaven! Those things are found in the capital city of the new earth—that's the New Jerusalem. We will live forever in the final kingdom that God establishes on the new earth with its capital, the New Jerusalem.

The New Jerusalem is described beginning in Revelation 20:16 where John gives the dimensions of the city. Then in verse 19, he says that the foundations of the city were garnished will all manner of precious stones. I have read commentaries with many different opinions about the shape of the city. Whatever the shape, John says the foundations are garnished with precious stones and he goes on to list some of those stones. Many people think of a foundation as unseen under ground, but you can see this foundation and the precious stones that garnish it. The walls of this city are 216 feet thick and there are 12 gates into this city. The city itself is a 1,500 mile square and 1,500 miles straight up. For the city to be 1,500 miles high, it would be twelve stories tall.

Do you realize that based on these figures, this city will be so large, it would stretch from Maine to Florida, from the Atlantic Ocean over 600 miles past the Mississippi River? That city—that one city—would cover over half of the United States. That is a massive city! With a city of that size, you can't get in mind that each gate of the city is 5 foot wide. The gates will be much larger than that. And each gate is made of one pearl. That pearl has got to be enormous!

If you take the square footage of the New Jerusalem and multiply it by 12, billions of people could inherit 640 acres just in the new Jerusalem. God is a massive God! Don't worry about overcrowding in heaven.

In verse 23, John gives more detail. He says the city has no need of the sun or the moon to shine in it because the glory of God will light the city and the Lamb is the light. Each story of that city will be illuminated with the glory of the presence of God.

If you think you and your group are the only ones going to this city, you'd better think again. God made that city a big place to house whosoever will. Whoever is thirsty, let them come and drink of the water of life freely. This is the New Jerusalem.

According to John's writings in Revelation, there will be no church there. John says the Lord God Almighty and the Lamb are the temple. Why is that? Because we are going to be living with the One we come to worship. We're going to be living with Him forever and ever.

The New Jerusalem is the residence of the bride, the Lamb's wife. In Revelation 19, we're introduced to the idea that there will be a marriage of the Lamb. Once the bride, the Church, becomes the wife of the Lamb, this is where the Church will reside forever with the Lamb.

When I was growing up, I always heard that when we get to heaven, we're going to bow down and worship God. There's no doubt we will do that, but we will do so much more. We're going to assume another life as we live forever with God. Look at Isaiah 65:17-18:

> *For, behold, I create new heavens and a new earth: and the former shall not be remembered, nor come into mind. But be ye glad and rejoice for ever in that which I create: for, behold, I create Jerusalem a rejoicing, and her people a joy.*

All three of the elements are mentioned here that are mentioned in Revelation 21: a new heaven, a new earth, and a New Jerusalem. This scripture obviously cannot be talking about the Jerusalem that exists now because the writer says, "I create Jerusalem." This tells me that everything that follow those words describes what will be in the new heaven and the new earth. Everything we read following those words flows into that. Continue in verse 19:

And I will rejoice in Jerusalem, and joy in my people: and the voice of weeping shall be no more heard in her, nor the voice of crying.

The writer of Isaiah is confirming everything we read in Revelation chapter 21 and 22. There will not be any pain, weeping, crying, or sorrow there. When God wipes tears out of your eyes, the loved ones that did not make it to heaven are not going to haunt you because you will forget they ever existed. Heaven will not be a place of fretting or falling apart. It will not be a place of depression. There is only joy and rejoicing. There will be no pressures there on your life. This is hard for us to grasp because our life is filled with pressure from waking to sleeping. We live under all kinds of pressures and obligations.

Let's go on to read in verse 20:

There shall be no more thence an infant of days, nor an old man that hath not filled his days: for the child shall die an hundred years old;

This passage throws many people off when they read it. They wonder if this is saying that children are going to die in the New Jerusalem. That is not what this is saying at all. The Jews calculated life in seven year cycles: from 0-7 is infancy; from 7-14 is childhood; from 14-21 is young adult. When you get to age 49, things start downhill. This verse says that a child will die at 100 years old. In the New Jerusalem, a child will still be a child at 100 years old.

My wife and I had a miscarriage between the birth of our two children. I never got to hold that miscarried baby, but when I get to heaven, the angel will put that child in my arms and I will live with that child from then on. Remember Christ said that if you have forsaken houses, family or lands, He will restore that to you a hundredfold. Every aborted baby is not lost because,it was a life, not a mere fetus. God has not lost a single one of those precious lives. They are all there with Him. If you made a mistake early in life and aborted a child, I believe you will raise that child when you get into the kingdom of God so don't fret about it. Heaven will solve all the problems and dilemmas we've ever run into.

For those who could never have children, have you ever wondered why? From all of the aborted babies who will be in heaven, God's going to furnish you with a family. He is good, kind and loving and He will bless you. God gave a command to multiply and populate the earth. The enemy came in and, through the curse, he made people barren. But it is the intended blessing of God that you bear children. In Matthew 19:29, Jesus says that if you have lost blessing, He will restore it to you a hundredfold and give you everlasting life. What a thrill and blessing!

Isaiah 65:20 goes on to say that "the sinner, being a hundred years old, shall be accursed." This gives us a comparison of heaven to hell. For those who are lost without God, time will drag on in torment as they are separated from God. They will know that they will never be freed from damnation.

Verse 21 says, "they shall build houses and inhabit them." You may be thinking that Jesus went to prepare a place for us, why would we be building? Jesus went to prepare the New Jerusalem, but you also have the new heaven and the new earth to fill. Look on to verses 21-22:

And they shall build houses, and inhabit them; and they shall plant vineyards, and eat the fruit of them. They shall not build, and another inhabit; they shall not plant, and another eat: for as the days of a tree are the days of my people, and mine elect shall long enjoy the work of their hands.

We're going to be busy when we get to heaven. That blesses me! You may be thinking, *I am worn out.* Just wait till you get your new body. When you get your new body, you'll never run out of steam and remember, there is no night there.

Verse 23 says that we will not labor in vain, for we are "the seed of the blessed of the LORD, and their offspring with them." That speaks of family. I'm a family oriented person. I love being around family. What a privilege that we will be with our offspring for eternity. God is a family minded God. After He had made nearly all of creation, He knew that it was good until he made man. After he made man, God said it was not good for man to be alone, so He made him a helpmate. God was the originator of family. He blessed and ordained it and intends for it to continue in the realm of His glory with the sanctifying power of God.

Genesis 25:8 says that when Abraham died, he was gathered unto his people. Genesis 25:17 says that Ishmael, Abraham's son, died and was gathered unto his people. Genesis 35:29 says that Isaac died and was gathered unto his people. Genesis 49:29 and 33 says that Jacob died and was gathered unto his people. Numbers 20:24 says that

Aaron died and was gathered unto his people. Judges 2:10 says that generation died and was gathered to their fathers. Ephesians 3:15 speaks of the whole family in heaven and earth. All of these things are important. If you don't believe there will be family in heaven, that's fine, but I have family I am looking forward to seeing. I have family I'm looking forward to being with as the years go by. They were very dear and precious to me and I'm looking forward to being with them.

Isaiah 65:24 says, "And it shall come to pass, that before they call, I will answer; and while they are yet speaking, I will hear." When we get into that kingdom, we will travel at the speed of thought. People talk about the speed of light but this says that before you even ask, it's going to be answered. We will travel at the speed of thought.

Isaiah 65:25 says, "The wolf and the lamb shall feed together, and the lion shall eat straw like the bullock: and dust shall be the serpent's meat. They shall not hurt nor destroy in all my holy mountain, saith the LORD." What a peaceful place that God is preparing for us.

When we get there, there will be great things for us to enjoy. We will enjoy the society of holy men of old: Abraham, Joseph, Moses, Joshua, David, Isaac, Daniel, Peter, John, Paul, all of these will be there. And also your loved ones and your family will be there.

Some have said that when they get to heaven, they have a lot of questions that they're going to ask. No you won't. You're not going to have any questions when you get there. When you change from the corruptible into the incorruptible, everything that you wondered or had questions about will automatically and immediately become clear at that time. Look at 1 Corinthians 13:9-13:

For we know in part, and we prophesy in part. But when that which is perfect is come, then that which is in part shall be done away.

When I was a child, I spake as a child, I understood as a child, I thought as a child: but when I became a man, I put away childish things. For now we see through a glass, darkly; but then face to face: now I know in part; but then shall I know even as also I am known. And now abideth faith, hope, charity, these three; but the greatest of these is charity.

Verse 12 says that now we are looking through a glass darkly. As you look through a dark glass, you make out images and have some idea of what's out there, but you can't see it clearly. But we are told that then we will see clearly, face to face. Now we know in part. Right now, I'm in the Bible every day, but I still have a lot of questions. But when I'm changed from the corruptible to the incorruptible, every question that I had will be answered at that time. Not only that, but such knowledge is going to be put in us that there will be no time of introducing. God's not going to spend the first million years introducing everybody. You'll just know them. Then shall you know even as you are known. There will be a day when Paul will come by and say, "Dean, I'm glad you made it." And I'll turn to him and say, "When I got into that book of Corinthians and looked at chapters 12, 13, and 14 where you explained about the gifts of the Spirit and what will happen when this life is over with, man didn't that help me!" I'll say to James, "That little old book you wrote, only 5 chapters but how powerful it was. When I learned about anointing with oil in the name of the Lord, man did that open everything up to me." We'll just sit and visit as time rolls by. What a day and a blessing that will be.

Questions arise such as what will we be like or what will our new body be like? Do you realize that people asked these same questions in the days of Paul? He told the Corinthians in 1 Corinthians 15:35, 38, 49:

> *But some man will say, How are the dead raised up? and with what body do they come? But God giveth it a body as it hath pleased him, and to every seed his own body. And as we have borne the image of the earthy, we shall also bear the image of the heavenly.*

Remember, Adam was made in the image and likeness of God. When Adam sinned, we lost the likeness of God, but we didn't lose the image of God. This passage is saying that our heavenly bodies will look something like they do now, but there will be no imperfections. We are all going to be perfected.

In Matthew 22, the Sadducees who do not believe in the resurrection of the dead, came to Jesus to ask him a hypothetical question. They asked Jesus, if there was a man who was married and had no children who then died, leaving his wife to marry his brothers until all died without having children, whose wife will she be in the resurrection? Jesus answers them by saying in verses 29-30 of chapter 22, "Ye do err, not knowing the scriptures, nor the power of God. For in the resurrection they neither marry, nor are given in marriage, but are as the angels of God in heaven." People read this and believe that this scripture is stating that there will not be family in heaven. That's not what this scripture says at all. This group of people posing the question to Jesus were wondering who was going to raise children by this woman when they get to heaven. That was the whole point of the story. Jesus states that we won't be giving birth in heaven, we'll be as the angels. The angels don't reproduce. When we get to heaven, the families that be, will be.

God made you spirit, soul, and body and in that order. Two parts of you are eternal and only one part is natural. 1 Thessalonians 5:23 says, "And the very God of peace sanctify you wholly; and *I pray God* your whole spirit and soul and body be preserved blameless unto the coming of our Lord Jesus Christ." It's amazing that the only part of you that's natural is what your biological parents gave you at birth. And it's the only part of you that God's going to change in the resurrection. Your soul and spirit are already eternal. They will either spend that eternity in hell or in heaven with Jesus Christ, but you are eternal in nature.

Why did God make us spirit, soul, and body? So that He could communicate with us. Only the Word of God can separate soul and spirit, but they are two separate entities. Hebrews 4:12 says, "For the word of God is quick, and powerful, and sharper than any twoedged sword, piercing even to the dividing asunder of soul and spirit, and of the joints and marrow, and is a discerner of the thoughts and intents of the heart." God separated the soul and spirit by His Word.

1 Corinthians 2:9-12 helps us discern the difference between soul and spirit.

But as it is written, Eye hath not seen, nor ear heard, neither have entered into the heart of man, the things which God hath prepared for them that love him. But God hath revealed them unto us by his Spirit: for the Spirit searcheth all things, yea, the deep things of God.

For what man knoweth the things of a man, save the spirit of man which is in him? even so the things of God knoweth no man, but the Spirit of God.

Now we have received, not the spirit of the world, but the spirit which is of God; that we might know the things that are freely given to us of God.

Three spirits are mentioned in verses 11-12: the spirit of man, the Spirit of God, and the spirit of the world. John 4:24 tells us that God is a Spirit and those who worship Him must worship in spirit and in truth. That's how God connects with you. God does not connect Spirit to body or Spirit to emotion, He connects Spirit to spirit. Your spirit is your knowing. It's your intellect. What knows the things of man? The spirit of man which is in him.

Psalm 42:1-6 teaches us that your soul is your emotions. Not every day do I feel "saved". I don't get out of bed every morning excited, feeling "saved". But every day I know I'm saved. That's why God communicates with you through your spirit, not your soul or emotions. You must establish your blessing from God on the Word of God because the Word of God is what speaks into your spirit. When God gives you a promise, find a scripture that deals with that promise. When you have that scripture that deals with that promise, when your chin starts to quiver and the goosebumps are gone and nobody is there to cheer you on, just open your Bible to see if the scripture still reads the same. If the Bible still reads the same, then you've based your prayer and your miracle on the Word of God, it doesn't matter if you've got chillbumps or your chin is quivering, you're still receiving something from God because you based your blessing on the eternal Word of Almighty God which never changes. That's how faith is inspired.

Your body without your soul and spirit is dead. The breath of God is the glue that holds the inner man to the body and when He calls His breath home, there's nothing to keep you together. You've been to funeral services of friends and family. Their body is there, but what made them laugh, what made them cry, what made them who they were is gone. When your soul and spirit leave the body, the body does not function at all. But God speaks to your "know-er" or your spirit man to let you know that you have passed from death unto life. Then your spirit man notifies your "feel-er", or your soul man. Then my soul man punches up through my body and before you know it, what I know, I'm now feeling and what I'm feeling, I'm expressing through this body as a praise and adoration to God. That's how God designed us to work. He speaks to you Spirit to spirit. Then your spirit speaks to your soul and before you know it, tears are flowing and you're bubbling inside because you have known a touch of the living God of heaven.

In 1 John 3:2 it says that we do not know what we will be like, but we will be like Him. This is talking about in the now. You will be like Him in your walk now. When you see Him in heaven, you're going to recognize Him. When we receive our new body, it will be eternal but we will still look something like what we do now. We are made in the image of God and this was not lost in the fall of man. We lost the likeness, but not the image.

When a person dies, before their funeral is ever planned or their body ever taken to a funeral home, before that body reaches a cemetery, that person has already reached paradise in the presence of God. The Apostle Paul gives us the word that when we are absent from this body, there is no in between. When we are absent from this body, we are present with God. The only thing death can do to the child of God is get you into the presence of God. When you know Whom you've believed in and know where you're at in the things of God, death won't bother you.

The first experience in death is you fall asleep and wake up in the beauty of God's grace. You'll be conscious that you've left behind the earthly body with all its weakness, sufferings and limitations and then you'll be aware that you're being transported swiftly toward the third heaven—the beautiful country, shining bright as the sun. You'll be in the new environment where the atmosphere is love. There's no discord or lack of harmony. You'll meet Jesus and He'll welcome you home. Then you'll meet loved ones who have gone on before you. You'll meet the patriots of old: the apostles, prophets and Christians of all ages. That is the promise God has made to us. It's worth sacrificing for, it's worth living for. It's real and it exists.

CPSIA information can be obtained
at www.ICGtesting.com
Printed in the USA
FFOW05n0013200915